"How do we make sense of our stories—that odd collection of puzzles and pain, risks and dreams, gifts and passions that make up our lives? In *Your Vocational Credo*, Dr. Loyd leads readers through a series of questions to craft their own vocational credos. Readers will not only be able to articulate their own *why*, but also *who* on earth they are here for. This book is a sure guide to anyone wanting to live with meaning."
Loren Kerns, associate dean, George Fox Evangelical Seminary

"Too often a cacophony of voices tempt us to wander directionless toward no real purpose. Deborah Loyd cuts through the chatter and offers practical, sage and brilliant guidance. She is the person I trust to mentor others to discover their true voice and authentic vocation—the *why* of our lives. This is an indispensable resource for leading others, and more importantly, finding our own way forward."
Trey Doty, executive director, Responder Life

"Hidden within the long unfolding story of our pain, passions, signature moments and longings lies a unique song that only you are meant to sing. This sagely writer can help you leave behind the mediocrity of a meandering, unexamined life and discover your God-given voice and the lyrics that are uniquely yours for the good of the world."
Daniel Steigerwald, coach, church planter, trainer, educator, writer

"I know of no other person who is more qualified to write a genuinely transformational book on vocation than Deborah Loyd. Through her work of contextualizing the gospel for younger generations, she understands how to teach and translate God's wisdom in such ways that lives are deeply changed and souls are given hope. I anticipate that *Your Vocational Credo* will become a classic in its field."
Christine Wood, author, educator, founder of the EPIC Leadership Center

"It's a joy to see a book written about how we can love the Lord our God with all our vocation. Wouldn't it be amazing if we could grasp that our vocations are holy, sacred and just as important as pastoring or work at a church? Deborah is just the right person to be writing on this—she doesn't write from theory but from living it out."
Dan Kimball, pastor, Vintage Faith Church, author, *They Like Jesus but Not the Church*

"Deborah Loyd is a genuinely remarkable woman. As such, she is perfectly suited to talk artfully about the destiny-shaping pursuit of finding one's personal calling and integrating it into life."
Alan Hirsch, author and activist

"Packed with wisdom, real stories, biblical grounding and practical exercises, *Your Vocational Credo* is a much-needed tool for individuals, groups, churches and organizations. I know it will call many to life."
Kathy Escobar, co-pastor of The Refuge, spiritual director and author of *Faith Shift*

"What I love about Deb Loyd's book: First, it can be read and used well by people of all ages, in all walks of life, who are willing to stretch to find their true selves. Second, while beautifully poetic in its language and form, it is also amazingly practical and down to earth. By the time you've read it, you know exactly what to do to effect the changes in your life that will bring you to a new phase of existence."
Rita Warren, board chair, Christian Associates International

"Dr. Deborah Loyd . . . is a woman whose leadership and mentoring is marked by sacrificial risk, by beating the odds, by plumbing personal pain, by giving up posses- sions and position, in order to walk with young people on the margins of society. . . . This is the kind of authentic leadership the world needs."
Kelly Bean, author of *How to Be a Christian Without Going to Church*

"This book addresses important shifts in culture as a generation seeks to rediscover vo- cation and calling rather than letting work be a means to an end. The reader should be warned, a vocational credo will upset the status quo and ignite personal transformation."
Kirk L. Wayman, business and leadership consultant, Wayman Consulting, associate pastor, Redding First Church of the Nazarene

"One of the most important things we can do for ourselves—and ultimately for others and for the world—is to know who we are and what our purpose is on this planet. *Your Voca- tional Credo* is a blueprint for making your way, and Loyd is a creative and gifted guide."
Steve Knight, cofounder of Transform Network

"I love this book for its practicality. If you want to move forward toward your deepest dreams, this book can help you take that next step."
Mark Scandrette, author of *Free*

"Whether you are young and just starting the vocational journey, or are later in life and discerning a new direction, *Your Vocational Credo* is an intensely practical guide designed to help you discover your *why* and live from a place of meaning and purpose. . . . Deborah Loyd offers rich experience, inspiration and tangible resources to bring clarity to your search for true vocation."
Karlene Clark, lead pastor, Wesley United Methodist Church, cofounder of Convergence

"*Your Vocational Credo* is a sage guide for those of us in the wilderness trying to sort out the story we find ourselves in. Dr. Loyd helps provide that guidance with unfiltered wisdom and generous grace."
Pam Hogeweide, author of *Unladylike*

"You couldn't ask for a better guide in asking that most personal and persistent of ques- tions: What am I doing with my one and only life?"
Brian D. McLaren, author, speaker, activist

Your Vocational Credo

*Practical Steps to Discover
Your Unique Purpose*

Deborah Koehn Loyd

IVP Books

An imprint of InterVarsity Press
Downers Grove, Illinois

InterVarsity Press
P.O. Box 1400, Downers Grove, IL 60515-1426
ivpress.com
email@ivpress.com

InterVarsity Press® is the book-publishing division of InterVarsity Christian Fellowship/USA®, a movement of students and faculty active on campus at hundreds of universities, colleges and schools of nursing in the United States of America, and a member movement of the International Fellowship of Evangelical Students. For information about local and regional activities, visit intervarsity.org.

All Scripture quotations, unless otherwise indicated, are taken from THE HOLY BIBLE, NEW INTERNATIONAL VERSION®, NIV® Copyright © 1973, 1978, 1984, 2011 by Biblica, Inc.™ Used by permission. All rights reserved worldwide.

While many stories in this book are true, some names and identifying information may have been changed to protect the privacy of individuals.

Cover design: Cindy Kiple
Interior design: Beth McGill
Images: © anfisa_focusova/iStockphoto

ISBN 978-0-8308-4319-0 (print)
ISBN 978-0-8308-9869-5 (digital)

Printed in the United States of America ∞

Library of Congress Cataloging-in-Publication Data
Loyd, Deborah Koehn, 1952-
  Your vocational credo : practical steps to discover your unique purpose / Deborah Koehn Loyd.
    pages cm
  Includes bibliographical references.
  ISBN 978-0-8308-4319-0 (pbk. : alk. paper)
  1. Vocation--Christianity. I. Title.
  BV4740.L695 2015
  248.4--dc23
                                                                      2015022992

P 21 20 19 18 17 16 15 14 13 12 11 10 9 8 7 6 5 4 3 2 1

Y 33 32 31 30 29 28 27 26 25 24 23 22 21 20 19 18 17 16 15

To Ken,

my partner and husband of thirty-six years,

who yet inspires me daily

with his passion for people.

Contents

Introduction

Welcome to the journey—your journey. This book is about noticing patterns, those that come from your own story, that mark you, shape who you are and help you to be your best self. Most of us are well acquainted with the events of our own stories, yet we have not made sense of the mountain peaks and valleys in them that form us. The trends and truths get lost in the multitude of clues that vie for our attention. The chatter distracts us and the landscape becomes flattened.

Christine and I met when we were studying in India. She was a ray of hope in a landscape that seemed void of mentors for someone like me. I begged her to mentor me, and she eventually said yes. Until I began my vocational exploration at Christine's urging, I had no idea how to interpret the events of my life. Since then, I have collected a few unconventional shortcuts that will help you to move along more quickly than I was able to. I offer you a process to help you read and interpret your own story. It includes developing your vocational credo and discovering ways that you might live it out. Your vocational credo describes why you are on earth and what you will do about it. You will adapt and re-adapt the concepts demonstrated in this book before you find the right words to describe you. Only then will the credo become truly yours.

In the following chapters you'll find your pathway forward by delving into these questions:

- What are the differences between vocation, career, job and calling?

- What are you all about? What is your ultimate *why*?

- What are your gifts, talents and tools?

- What are the personal barriers to success that will keep you from living into your vocation?

- How has pain been formative in your story, and what does it contribute to your vocation?

- What in your past is waiting to be energized?

> Vocation is a creative significant work unique to you, expressed with deep joy as a love offering to God, exuding self-respect and care for others that meets the needs of the world in a meaningful way.

- In what ways does your greatest joy intersect with the deep needs of the world?

- What is your greatest hope?

- How do you establish enduring significance for your life's work? How does it live on after you are gone?

Furthermore, vocation rests on three pieces of hard work. The first is to discover what you are all about. This is the journey of your *why*, which is shorthand for a question that most of us have asked at one time or another, Why do I exist? Your responses to the preceding questions will help you to begin to form that answer. The second piece is discovering how to make yourself available to God in a way that makes sense to you. This requires your commitment to explore how you will utilize your skills, gifts and talents in life-giving ways for yourself and others. The third element comes from my mother, who, at a very dark time in my life, gave me this sage bit of advice: "We don't do faith *if* it works. We do faith *until* it works. This is what spirituality is all about." She helped me understand that trial and error are part of the process. I learned that what I did not fight for could never be mine. Numerous times this advice has

> The place God calls you to is the place where your deep gladness and the world's deep hunger meet.
> FREDERICK BUECHNER[1]

helped me to flow with my circumstances, rather than fight them, and find my way to success. As it turns out, it is crucial to know when to fight and when not to fight.

By applying the practices in this book you will develop an inner voice that will gain strength. And as that happens God will respond with enablement and opportunity. It is a circular proposition: You risk, God shows up, you respond, and then it starts over again. Accepting a lifestyle that welcomes risk and does not shrink from failure is the cornerstone of growth. If you make yourself available, God will give you opportunities to do what you do best and the capacity to do it with maximum effectiveness.

So I write this book with three assumptions. First, everyone has a unique vocation that God desires for each of us to fulfill. Second, our fulfillment in life is tethered to the discovery and performance of our vocation. Third, vocation is meant to be altruistic, that is, for the sake of others. Without others, vocation deteriorates to narcissism.

What if God is so generous that God cannot help but give each human being a vocation that will contribute to changing the world? It is possible for everyone, from teenagers to retirees, to find our significant vocation because God intends for us to find it. Vocation creates people who love what they do and who inspire others to be more than they currently are. People with passion will never lack for vision or mission. Neither will they lack for followers. What kind of greatness is hiding in you? Are you willing to find out? You may become the hero in your own story!

> I am particularly passionate to show that altruism and compassion are not luxuries, but essential needs to answer the challenges of our modern world.
>
> MATTHIEU RICARD,
> "The World's Happiest Man"[2]

A LITTLE OF MY BACKSTORY

My journey to discover my vocation could not have happened without my partner in crime, Ken, my husband of thirty-six years, and my amazing children and grandchildren. When Ken and I were first married, we worked at jobs that paid the bills but were unfulfilling on most levels. Both being raised by parents from a generation that emphasized responsibility over fulfillment, we responded well to their tutelage but found ourselves feeling stuck. Once we dared to step outside of the norm, we began to dream, and based on those dreams we took risks, lots of them. Life changed dramatically. The ride became extremely bumpy and at the same time crazy exciting.

In the 1990s we started a church for twentysomethings. It was unlike anything that had come before it. Edgy did not even begin to describe it. What a wild ride that was! Ken has since started three churches for our friends who live outdoors in Portland, Oregon. I went back to school for ten years and became a college professor. I went on to partner in a couple of organizations to empower Christian women: Women's Convergence and Women's Theology Hub. I now work with Forge, an organization that supports those who want to live missionally as well as young church planters. I also started Finding Forward, which is my ongoing endeavor to help people find their vocation. I do retreats, group training, individual coaching and certified training.

For Ken and me there is no turning back to the staid life of the past. Our friends suggest that we think about retirement, but that doesn't sound right just yet. Although we now are grandparents and in the legacy season of our lives, we continue to change and grow, finding new ways to express our vocations. As it turns out, God is not finished with us yet.

The impetus for this body of research and this book is a result of my loss of voice. This occurred on two levels. The first was the virtual loss of voice that happened through sexual abuse. Fear and shame robbed me of my ability to tell my own story. My abuser threatened me into silence. This signaled a self-destructive urge within me that took years to unravel through therapy and working out my spirituality.

The second loss of voice was quite literal. I developed a condition called spasmodic dysphonia, which left me with barely a whisper. My life dramatically altered as a result of this loss, creating a domino effect of losses in other areas. It was also the very thing that set me on my journey to find healing, vocation and a more gracious view of God. My story has been miraculous, and I trust that yours will be too.

I desire that everyone, especially those reading this book, will find that sweet spot of vocation for their lives. I want you to be able to say as I have, "I never dreamed that life with God could be this exciting!" And "If you would have told me thirty years ago about all the amazing things I would experience, I *never* would have believed you."

My prayer is that you will be filled with wonder as you discover your own wild frontier! Cheers to God from whom all blessings flow, and cheers to you as you begin the journey!

1

Why Vocation Matters

It was autumn 1969 and career day at my high school. Students sat with eager anticipation, hoping to answer with some imagination the questions that were posed: To which career do you feel called? What would you like to do for the rest of your life? My friends chose careers that sounded interesting and planned for either vocational school or college after graduation. I was perplexed. The questions did not seem right to me. Although I didn't dare say it out loud, inside my head I was screaming, *Nothing! I do not want to do any one thing for the rest of my life!* For some reason the idea of a career seemed boring, lifeless and not a legitimate way to express the real me. I understood career as something similar to the electrical wiring in the house. People need electricity, but who wants to focus on wires and electrical current when there are lamps, radios, movies and music to be explored and enjoyed? Better that the mundane functioning systems be hidden behind the walls, enabling us to focus on the important things.

The idea of making money and supporting myself, much like those wires, felt important, but it seemed like it should be secondary to more passionate inspiration and dramatic events. The future was a mysterious, unknown drama that held many possibilities yet to be played out, including the journey of self-discovery. Yet I felt pressed to become a cog in the machine, to choose a job and do my part methodically, contributing to society until I struck it rich or retired, whichever came first. Inside my head I was functioning more like a method actor, asking myself, *What is my motivation here?* I wanted to make a difference. I wanted a reason to *become* something and a purpose beyond the mundane. I wanted an inspired, exciting future.

When the career specialist finally rolled out my choices, I was underwhelmed, to say the least. My options were limited: teacher (Same room, same kids every day? No thanks), nurse (Sorry, can't do blood), librarian ("Disturbs Others" was commonly checked on my grade school report card so this was not a natural fit), secretary (I was independent and self-determined, no bossy boss for me), seamstress (Who can sit in one place for that long?), and stewardess (Well, that one was intriguing, just impractical if I ever wanted a family). This was an era when the typewriter was a woman's domain, a man in the nursing profession would be considered effeminate and stewardesses (there were no stewards or flight attendants back then) could not be married. Men's and women's roles were rigidly defined, and the career specialist's suggestions reflected this limiting fact.

My mother had raised my expectations with a worldview that was ahead of her time and apparently mine too. "You do not have to be a secretary; you can be the boss. You do not have to be a nurse; you can be the doctor." My mother had inspired me with these thoughts, and I believed her with all my heart. Once I left home I struggled unsuccessfully to find mentors who had horizons beyond the norm. There was no one to tell me "You can do better than this" or "Take some time to explore your options" or most importantly,

"What are *you* all about? What really excites you? Where do you find meaning?"

And then there was the spiritual side of the struggle. From my Catholic upbringing I knew that God had made me a unique individual. I sensed that I was born to do something that no one else could do. If this was true, why did it feel like I had to wrestle with God to find out what my vocation, my life's work, would be? Why was it such a big secret? Later on I became a good Pentecostal. I knew how to obey. If I thought God said, "Do it," I did it no matter how crazy "it" seemed. I was convinced that obedience was not the issue. Discerning God's will was the problem. *Just tell me what to do!* was my simplistic prayer. But it seemed as if the heavens were turning away my prayers like the clouds on a gray day in Seattle turn away the brilliant rays of the sun.

What I didn't know back then was that no matter how much I prayed, the answer would not emerge from prayer or merely choosing a career or doing what was convenient. Vocation would not fall into my lap. The pathway forward would become a spiritual journey that included much more than I could imagine. Puzzle pieces would emerge from loving but honest conversations with friends and mentors. Books would shed light on the path. Movies, art and music, each in their own way, would enliven my search. Discerning the themes and trajectories of my life would take on a life of its own. I would learn to lean into my most painful moments, discovering passion that was hidden in the darkness of my pain. Hour after hour of sitting and prayerfully examining my life in the light of God's wisdom, grace and provision would paint a picture into which all those puzzle pieces would be integrated. And through all of this, my pathway forward would emerge and my vocation would come to light.

Since that time I have walked down the pathway of vocational discernment with many friends, family members, students, business colleagues and clients. I am more convinced than ever that every individual has a specific vocation that can be coaxed out and brought to light through patience, probing and reflection. Finding vocation is an act of spiritual practice that must be cherished and held reverently. It is not withheld from us. Rather through exploration, self-knowledge and the gentle guidance of the Holy Spirit, vocation is revealed in us. However, like most treasures, we must search diligently to find it.

THE POWER OF PURPOSE

Dr. Viktor Frankl, Holocaust survivor, psychiatrist and creator of logotherapy, observed in the Nazi concentration camp that those who had the ability to hope in the future were able to rally the courage to weather the unendurable.[1] Frankl said,

> Everyone has his own specific vocation or mission in life: everyone must carry out a *concrete assignment* which demands fulfillment. Therein he cannot be replaced, nor can his life be repeated. Thus, everyone's task is unique as is his specific opportunity to implement it.[2]

Frankl noticed that those living in the most deprived and debasing circumstances could survive if their lives had meaning and purpose. These were the keys to dignity, hope and survival. Vocation is what brings substance, meaning and purpose to the events of life, whether we understand these events or not. In Frankl's case, his mission was to be reunited with his loved ones. Although Frankl's entire family died in the camps, he was able, in spite of profound disappointment and loss, to press on to a future of good work, prosperity, love and long life. And in the process he found vocational fulfillment doing the work of a psychiatrist and researcher.

Each one of us is put on earth for a unique purpose. The apostle

Paul writes, "We are God's handiwork, created in Christ Jesus to do good works, which God prepared in advance for us to do" (Ephesians 2:10). This is a teleological plan, meaning a plan with an end in mind. God's story for you and me is a story of purpose. Although none of us can predict the future, we are safe trusting the trajectory that God has allowed in our lives, because it will enable us to do the good works that God intends for us to do. However, if we ultimately fail to accomplish that purpose, there is no other human being that can fulfill the assignment in place of us. It is an intriguing and sobering thought that I have been designed specifically to fulfill a particular role on earth in a way no one else can. This realization gives birth to the perspective that vocation is a spiritual practice. Partnership with God is absolutely necessary.

Our Holy Book reminds us that our lives are not ours alone, but we are given to this world to serve others. We cannot do this without the help of God. I am guessing that you might share the same idea. God's mercy and love engulf us completely as we search to find purpose and its resulting responsibility. Because of the cross, our mistakes and missteps are forgiven even before they happen. God is glorified when I become the best me that I can be. My unique expression of God is a testimony to the goodness and breadth of my Creator. In accepting my uniqueness I am able to support the unique gifts of others.

Vocation is speaking or living forth the truest form of self. Vocation does not merely happen to us from the outside in a blinding light from heaven or an official "call" from God. That sweet spot of significance suited only to you must be discovered from the inside as well. A thorough inner exploration is necessary because it will allow you to bring your most energized and creative self into the future. It will ignite passion in your soul that is specific to you. When that passion collides with God-given opportunity, you have the elements of vocation and the power to change the world. Who wouldn't want that?

DON'T BE LEFT BEHIND

Passion: zeal that sustains energy to accomplish goals.

My story is not unique. It took me a long time, a lifetime, to discover my vocation, which is to help others find their voice both literally and vocationally. But it doesn't have to be that way for everyone. In fact most young people launching careers today cannot afford it to be that way. We live in compelling times that demand our attention and energy. It is easy to be left behind. The problem is that the world is changing so fast it is difficult to know how to respond for survival, let alone addressing meaning in life. Before 2002, Gordon Moore, the cofounder of Intel, determined that the processing speed of a computer chip doubled every eighteen months, accelerating the ability to disseminate information.[3] YouTube videographers Karl Fisch, Scott McLeod and Laura Bestler suggested that in 2006 technical information was doubling every two years, and by 2010 it was expected to double every seventy-two hours.[4] Guess what! We have passed that now.

Shift Happens, an informative video presentation by Fisch, McLeod and Jeff Brenman, gives a view of the unprecedented challenges for the job seeker:

- The top ten jobs in 2010 did not exist in 2004.

- Students are currently preparing for jobs that will use technologies not yet invented in order to solve problems we don't even know are problems yet.

- The US Department of Labor estimates that today's learner will have ten to fourteen jobs by the age of thirty-eight.

- One in four workers has been with their current employer for less than one year, and one in two for less than five years.

- Many of today's college majors didn't exist ten years ago. These include new media, organic agriculture, e-business, nanotechnology and homeland security.

- For students starting a four-year technical degree this means that half of what they learn in their first year of study will be outdated by their third year of study.[5]

How are we to keep up with this bewildering rush of change? Career sustainability is a moving target these days. How do these pieces fit together for the graduate? Yet, in the midst of this career uncertainty, I have never met so many young people who want to change the world but just don't know how to go about it. This is a crisis of vocation. And adding insult to injury, the educational bar has been raised. Where once a bachelor's degree was required to be competitive in the marketplace, now a master's degree or a PhD is needed just to be eligible. Does the need for higher education draw us toward our purpose or distract us from it? This remains to be seen.

Tony Campolo and Bruce Main give the reader pause in their book *Revolution and Renewal*. They write about the vocational benefits of a program called Mission Year, which engages the youth and energy of college students to transform cities. Campolo says,

> For students who haven't got a clue about what to do with their lives, it can be a defining experience to take a year off from school and get involved in a ministry that brings them into constant contact with some of the most socially disad-

vantaged and oppressed people in America. Time and time
again, listening to and praying with people in need helps
these students to grapple with what their own lives mean. In
more cases than not, unfocused young people come away
from this year of missionary service with clarity about their
vocational choices.[6]

As these students gave themselves wholeheartedly to mission,
they were able to see what was important for their own futures.
When faced with compelling needs, young people quickly found
their resonance. They discovered what was calling out to them and
where their passion was leading. It would be amazing if all college
students could have life-altering experiences like those in Campolo's program, centering them on their life's vocation while still in
the formative process. Rather than taking merely convenient
courses of study or someone else's idea of what they should study,
students could choose majors that more closely reflect their passions. What if more students were aided in finding their vocations
sooner and subsequently changed the world? What if they were
able to become what they hoped for? Vocation has a transformative
element to it that draws its seekers into permanent change.

Although the college years have passed for many of us, finding
vocation is not only possible but gives many elders a vitality for life
they have never known to be possible. Older adults have advan-
tages that younger people don't. They have learned how to per-
severe and know what works for them. Older adults are often more
financially secure and have time to give. These allow more choices
and opportunities for vocational expression. The latter years can be
more exciting than the former. If you are like me, you want to
change the world. Sometimes my sixty-plus years try to convince
me that I am too old for this endeavor. But if not now, then when?

Time is running out. I have a passion for an authentic gut-inspired voice that exudes from deep within my soul. If you are like me, this book is for you too. Everyone deserves to be heard. In the symphony of voices, wisdom, creativity and future will be found.

Oliver Wendell Holmes Sr. said, "Many people die with their music still in them. Too often it is because they are always getting ready to live. Before they know it time runs out."[7] Who wants to leave this world without offering their contribution to the symphony? Grandma Jerri, a little lady I knew, was dying of lung cancer. She clung to her cigarettes and her Gameboy until her very last breath. My heart broke for her—and for all of us. She died without singing her song. I can't seem to forget her. I wonder about the beauty inside of Grandma Jerri that she never managed to share with the world. What passion inside of you is waiting to be ignited? How will you express it? What if we all, young and old, found our voices sooner and changed the world together? Not doing so is too great a risk when the world needs us.

WHAT ARE YOU ALL ABOUT?

In the movie *The Cider House Rules* Arthur Rose, the orchard boss, has a confrontation with his underlings who are threatening to overwhelm his authority.[8] Angrily he yells, "What are you all about? 'Cause I'm about apples. What are you about?" In their violent world the question was important. His pointed clarity forced the crew to focus on that one motivation that would guide their future behavior and possibly their survival. Although I think Arthur missed the point in some ways, his ability to exact that kind of focus, first from himself and then from his crew, was inspiring and thought provoking. He was a strong leader who caused his men to dig deep for that which was relevant in the moment. The scene reminded me of a conversation I had long ago with a mentor who pressed me to answer a few questions about my voice, which I was struggling to discover: What keeps you awake at night? What brings you to tears? What makes you angry?

My mentor may as well have asked me the color of a C chord on my guitar. The questions barely made sense. At the time I knew I was not equipped to answer her questions by myself. I wanted help, which she wisely would not offer. She wanted me to ruminate on the questions and struggle for my own answers, no matter how long it took me. These life-defining questions were meant to cause me to carefully consider the thrust of my education and how I would spend my future. I needed to discover what made my own heart beat. Each of us has a heart meant to beat in symphony with the Holy Spirit. Although I knew that from sermons I had heard, I still could not put my finger on what that was for me. As I began to consider my gifts, talents and the tools I had acquired, I realized that I had to approach this journey as a spiritual practice. Self-examination, reflection and reverence would be my traveling buddies. I thought, *Good, I've got six months before school starts. I can get this done.* I knew neither how deep I would have to dig nor how long it would take to get there. Before I knew it, six months turned into six years. So there is no better time than the present to begin the journey.

REFLECTION AND PRACTICE

Vocation is something that we would do whether or not there was a paycheck. It is a passion that exudes from our soul and transcends any particular job or career we may find ourself in. Vocation brings joy in the midst of tedium and normal. It is simple and profound, hidden and obvious, natural and spiritual. I define *vocation* as *a creative, significant work expressed with deep joy as an offering of love to God, self and others that meets the needs of the world in a meaningful way.*

Reflect on these questions and note your responses.

1. What do you think your vocation might be in light of my definition?

2. What keeps you awake at night?

3. What brings you to tears?

4. What makes you angry?

5. What would you be compelled to do even if there was no paycheck associated with it?

What Is
Vocation Anyway?

Eleanor Roosevelt said, "It is not more vacation that we need—it is more vocation."[1] Mrs. Roosevelt was hinting that a calling would bring greater refreshment to the soul than time spent away from one's employment. An occupation could be revitalizing if it was the right work. Furthermore, if we chose the right career, our job could be a real vocation and thus be fulfilling.

I am sorry, was that last paragraph a little confusing? It should have been. Have you noticed how many words are used for what we do to make money and otherwise occupy our working selves: *vocation, calling, career, employment, work, occupation* and *job.* I used all seven of them in the first paragraph. To understand the nuances of vocation, we must discuss a few words that are often used interchangeably. Too often these words are assumed to be the same as *vocation.* Most of them are not. However, there is some crossover in meaning. I will focus only on *job, work, career, calling* and *vocation* so as not to belabor the point. Let's take a few minutes to tease out the differences between them and thus lessen the confusion.

IT'S JUST A JOB

Leon is an in-house accountant at an insurance agency where he has worked for four years. At the end of last quarter, as he was about to put the tax reports in the mail, he remembered a substantial amount of income that he had failed to include on the report. The tax form and the check were already in the stamped and sealed envelope and ready to go. Leon contemplated redoing the report, which would have been proper protocol according to tax law. However, it was a Friday and nearly time to head for home for a few well-deserved days off. Leon ruminated, *I'm tired and I don't want to waste a stamp. I'll just fix it next quarter. It's not that big of a deal.* In an effort to soothe his guilty conscience, he mumbled "It's just a job" as he slipped the envelope into the mail slot and headed out the door.

A *job* is a group of homogeneous tasks related by similarity of function. Leon's job was handling the cash flow, financial reporting and taxes for the insurance company. Jobs are most often performed by an employee and rarely done without pay. As Leon's story demonstrates, a job is generally not associated with passion or meaning. Leon said, "It's just a job," meaning that it pays the bills without providing deep significance. Although we generally associate a *job* with working at McDonald's, I have interviewed highly paid influential people who told me that what they do is just a job. Leon was well-respected and well-compensated for his work, but his job lacked the significance that would help him feel connected at a deeper level to those around him or to his inner longings. He could not imagine how this job connected him to God, and there was no attitude of reverent service. There was no trajectory for Leon's aspirations, hopes or dreams, evident in the way his job was playing out for him. Although the job provided financially for

Leon's family, his longings for significance were not being addressed, and Leon felt it. As a result he was not motivated to go the extra mile.

WHISTLE WHILE YOU WORK

Bruce was tinkering with something in his front yard as I approached. He had two plots of soil no more than five feet square in front of his modest condo. He had utilized every bit of the real estate with hearty plants below and hanging floral baskets and birdhouses above. Small as his yard was, Bruce also had a squirrel invasion. I could see that he was in his creative right-brain mode by the twinkle in his eyes. "I'm just having some fun out here!" was his comment. "You have to see this contraption that I made." He self-contentedly smiled from ear to ear. Relocating squirrels was his task for the day. The city required euthanasia for the animals, but in an act of compassion Bruce had fashioned a trap with duct tape, cardboard and some wood that allowed him to capture them and ferry the invaders to a forest outside of the city. This was not uncommon for Bruce, who at eighty-eight no longer allows others to determine his ways. Bruce is always doing something interesting and slightly subversive.

Bruce is a soft-spoken, gentle man who loves to work. Although retired, he is seldom at rest. Bruce thoroughly enjoyed his work in the aerospace industry, where he was employed for over three decades. After retirement his work took on a different timbre. He is not compensated for his work these days, in fact, it costs him money, but that doesn't matter to him. He enjoys the work of inventing useful mechanical devices, such as squirrel traps. And as the *go-to* guy of his condo, Bruce has become indispensable to his neighbors, many of whom are immigrants who do not understand American conventions, either social or mechanical. He has helped them buy cars, fix toilets and solve electrical problems, and has escorted a few of them to the emergency room.

Work, as Bruce demonstrates, has little to do with the typical understanding of a job, as described earlier with Leon. *The Oxford Dictionary* defines *work* as an "activity involving mental or physical effort done in order to achieve some result." This hints at intention. Ira Progoff, in his book *At a Journal Workshop,* deepens our understanding of work:

> It does not refer merely to a job that you have to do or to a task that is placed as a burden upon you. Having work implies a strong and warm caring, a special interest and concern. It means to be engaged in an activity which you value as something meaningful and valuable in your life, and which you are seeking to enlarge and to strengthen. A work is a specific project that emerges as an outer activity drawn from an inner source in a person's life.[2]

Progoff's definition infuses work with depth and growth. Progoff believes that work can take on almost any dimension, with possibilities as varied as humanity. What emerges in Bruce's work is the desire to be useful by helping others, human or otherwise, especially those who feel out of place, such as immigrants and squirrels. He draws from a deep inner well of goodwill. He cares about the quality of life for those around him and will do what he can to make life better for each person that crosses his path. His benevolence and love of life substantially anchor him to those around him. As Bruce's story demonstrates, the common threads of his work are personal meaning, care for others and a commitment to the project at hand. Work is very similar to vocation in that it finds needs and fulfills them according to a person's gifts and interests. Although life-defining in the immediate sense, it does not address the broader picture of one's life or one's passion. It does not ask the question, What am I here to do that only I can do?

A CAREER TRAJECTORY

"How is the most beautiful woman in the world?" That was my greeting when I walked through the door of the salon. Although such a comment could be perceived as patronizing, it was not. Stephanie has a way of making every person that spends time in her presence feel like a million bucks. It is her gift. Everyone is beautiful in some way, and she takes notice and talks about it.

Stephanie works as a hairdresser, a dreadlock artist to be specific. Although she claims to be backwards when it comes to business, she has carefully and intentionally built her client base and business practices. She is always on the search for new techniques and products in order to give her clients the best service possible. She cares about dreadlocks and about people. Clients fly in from across the country to sit in her chair, which provides opportunities for storytelling and laughs. Stephanie is dedicated to changing the typically gossip-ridden culture that is the norm for the beauty industry into an atmosphere of caring, acceptance and admiration, at least in her space. Stephanie's gifts of hospitality and affirmation, as well as her technical acumen, are the tools of her trade.

Career is defined as a dedication to an occupation for a significant amount of time with the opportunity for expansion and growth. Most commonly a career is a trajectory that builds on a person's job history, which has been consistently nurtured into a cohesive body of work.[3] Although Stephanie is only thirty-four years old, one-third of her life has been dedicated to her career path. Stephanie has become restless. She has hopes that her dreadlock business will become a steppingstone to something deeper. She has a longing to move beyond an industry that only allows intermittent interpersonal connections. Perhaps she will become a therapist. The gifts that have been nurtured in her via the salon experience, as well as the business tools that she has acquired, will support her next incarnation of self. Although she knows a change is coming, she has yet to zero in on what it might be.

The sweet spot happens when career and vocation overlay each other. Every college student hopes that career and vocation will turn out to be one and the same, a lifelong commitment to a work involving their passion. This often does not occur. Although some jobs lead a student away from their degreed course of study and successfully land them in their vocation, it is more common for career trajectories to veer off course and take the worker some place he or she had not intended to go. Or the person may be misplaced to begin with. How many students are doing work they never studied for? I have interviewed quite a few. Vocation drives one toward an ultimate purpose. It asks, What am I all about? How does this relate to my higher purpose and my fellow human beings? Stephanie finds meaning in her work, but she continues to look for the next incarnation of self. She searches for that thing that only she can give to the world.

ARE CALLING AND VOCATION THE SAME?

When I picked up the phone, Theresa was on the other end of the line. "I just can't do the church thing anymore. I know I am called to serve the church, but I've played flute on the worship team for years and it just feels stale. I am tired of volunteering in the nursery. And the prayer meetings are during my work hours. It all leaves me high and dry anyway. I think I am done serving at the church. And that makes me feel so unspiritual and guilty." The dejection and shame in her voice was startling, and yet I knew exactly how she felt. Finding your place in the cogs of a large church is next to impossible, unless you are one of the bright stars who rises to the top with a skill that the church needs. And how many of those are there—ten, maybe twelve per church? Sometimes folks know what their vocational contribution to the world is and become successful at what they do with or without the approval of church leadership. It is not uncommon for church leadership to feel competitive with or threatened by ministries that thrive outside of the four walls of the church. So then what are the rest of us to do? Consider Ken's story. He is an example of someone who went outside of the confines of the church to express his vocation.

On any Wednesday night you will find Ken in the midst of over one hundred homeless kids and young adults age twenty-five and under. He is feasting and laughing with them, while enjoying stories of their most recent exploits. A local church has given them shelter for one evening a week for their meal. On this particular night Ken stood up and shouted above the din of the crowd, "Hey! If anyone gets caught using drugs in here, not me but the community will throw you out! We love each other here, and so we do what is right by each other." This is as close to a sermon as he got that night at the Underground, a church for the young homeless in Portland, Oregon.

Ken has experienced a "call." Although if you ask him to tell the story of his call to ministry, he will deny that it happened. He tells it this way, "I just saw hurting people and wanted to help them feel better, so we do nothing special all the time. We just hang out and hopefully people will experience an oasis of warmth in an otherwise cold existence. They deserve to be loved just because they exist." Although Ken is deeply introverted, he comes alive at the Underground. Ken has started four churches, three for the homeless community, whom he calls "my friends who live outdoors." Ken smirks as he says, "My former pastor told me that I have gone further without talent than anyone he knows." Although Ken seems talented enough to me, it is clear that passion, not talent, is his main driver. Ken loves homeless kids, which comes from a deep well of pain that erupts from his own rejection as a child. He says that he has never felt wanted, and so he resonates with the kids on the street, those who "barely appear to themselves." He believes that if these kids feel wanted by at least one person, it will change the trajectory of their lives and they will begin to dream again. He has seen it work. Many of these young people grow into successful futures that they dreamed of but never imagined were possible. He longs for the traditional church to learn what he knows. Ken says he will be "creating communities for the abandoned and marginalized until the day he dies." And no doubt he will. Ken's vocational credo looks something like this: Ken was put on earth by God to pay attention to unwanted humans and to change the mind and heart of the church about the disenfranchised so both can benefit from knowing each other.

So what elements are noticeable in Ken's story that are not obvious in the others? Remember that Frederick Buechner describes vocation in this way: "The place God calls you to is the place where your deep gladness and the world's deep hunger meet."[4] That intersection of gladness and hunger is plainly more visible in Ken's ministry than anyone else I know, perhaps because it is so literally true for Ken and his crew.

The obvious difference between Ken's and Theresa's experiences is the way in which each understands *calling*. Theresa was an obedient servant of her faith community and jumped in where she was needed. She faithfully stretched herself for the sake of the church community for many years, but since much of her activity did not utilize her primary gifts or, more importantly, her passion, she became discouraged and quit. All the way around it was a poor fit. The idea of discovering her deep gladness was absent, and there was no one from her church who understood the importance of passion. Since that phone call Theresa has been through a vocational discernment workshop. She has become a popular artist in action for churches and conferences. Her vocational credo sounds something like this: Theresa was put on earth by God to help others to be formed spiritually and find joy, both through making art.

In contrast to Theresa, dramatic events catapulted Ken out of the traditional church setting and into a place where his passion could flourish. As it turns out, some folks are called to the margins, where they find others who are neither welcome in the traditional church nor comfortable there. Sometimes mainstream churches don't know how to help the severely broken. Some churches are frightened by those who are dirty, hungry and smell bad. Some churches don't want cross-dressers, murderers or alcoholics. Our church was not willing to invite these folks in. It was evident that we, as leaders, were misfits for this suburban community. Our pastor suggested that it was time for Ken and me to do whatever energized us. Ken found the hurting and disenfranchised wherever he went, be it the coffee shop, the local music store or on the street. He attracted them like flies to honey, and it was his joy to provide a safe space for these folks to flourish. Today both Theresa and Ken are living their vocations extravagantly.

THE BIBLICAL PERSPECTIVE ON CALLING

"If God has called you once, you are called forever. God never goes back on his word!" the preacher thundered from the pulpit. Tears began to leak from Sue's eyes. From the back pew of the church Sue wondered what had gone wrong. How had she failed? Did she not hear correctly? Was she not called? Her thoughts filtered back to that day when, as a twelve-year-old girl, she had responded to a call to Nigeria. She planned to go to nursing school and then move to Africa to live out her days as a medical missionary. But her own ill health had brought her home prematurely. At age thirty-two she was now questioning her call, *Am I no longer useful to God? What did I do to ruin my call?* She examined her heart prayerfully. Soon Sue would discover that nothing was wrong with her or her experience that an accurate view of calling could not clear up.

The confusion suffered by Sue was rooted in a misconception similar to Theresa's. Shame where no shame is due is often the result of bad interpretation of biblical words or religious ideas that we foster within Christian circles. As you might well guess, this problem of misinterpretation has a history. In his book *The Call*, Os Guinness tells us that this problem began hundreds of years ago with the Puritans. "Slowly such words as work, trade, employment and occupation came to be used interchangeably with calling and vocation."[5] We have reason to be confused. If *work* and *vocation* become interchangeable, we have no nuanced verbal tools with which to describe the variety of experiences or levels of commitment toward those experiences. And how do we describe the role of the Holy Spirit in vocational discernment? Using the right words becomes very important. So let's take a look at what troubles us.

Our English word *call* comes from the Latin word *vocatio*, which means a "call," a "summons" or an "invitation."[6] In the Bible it is used to mean a bidding forward into an act or practice of faith. The word *vocation* comes from the same cognate and means "a calling."[7] They are very similar, but historical distance has damaged their relationship to one another. *Calling* and *vocation* are sisters born of a common mister, and it would seem that they should be interchangeable. But as it turns out, current usage causes them to be more like brothers from different mothers. *Calling* has an otherworldly feeling to it. Today we use this word to describe a bidding that comes from outside of oneself, usually from God, for spiritual purposes such as missions and pastoring. In comparison, *vocation* has taken on the meaning of what one does to support the family and pay the bills. Vocational schools teach job trades. In education when one takes the vocational route it means he or she will be trained in welding, carpentry, food service or other manual jobs. In the end, the interpretation of *vocation* and *calling*, which were once interchangeable, is bifurcated. One is spiritual and the other is natural. One answers to God and the other to financial responsibility. One is imbued with deep meaning; the other not so much.

A MORE ACCURATE VIEW

God's people are *called* to work in harmony with the Holy Spirit (*vocation*) rather than to merely earn a paycheck. Working for a paycheck is admirable and necessary, but no matter what a person does for sustenance, vocation is possible. This concept will unfold as we move along. As we saw in the previous stories and definitions, the word *calling* has been co-opted through time to mean something other than its meaning in the Scriptures. As a result people are confused by the Scripture rather than being helped forward in their understandings of God's call on their lives. How does the Bible describe *calling*? If we use the Greek word in place of our translated English word, we can denude the original word of its adapted cultural connotations by allowing the original context to contribute to its actual meaning. The apostle Paul used *kaleō* to describe a bidding forward into a new way of life (Romans 11:29; 1 Corinthians 1:26; Ephesians 1:18). Believers were *kaleō*-ed to a pure walk, the high road and the work of faith (Philippians 3:14; 2 Thessalonians 1:11; 2 Timothy 1:9). Peter *kaleō*-ed believers to embody the divine nature (2 Peter 1:4-10). The author of Hebrews *kaleō*-ed the people to a heavenly expression of life on earth by following Jesus' example (Hebrews 3:1). By examining the context of *kaleō*, it becomes evident that *kaleō* is indeed a bidding or a compelling forward, in this case, into a deeper faith walk with Christ. So how did the meaning of *kaleō* morph from a spiritual exercise of faith lived in harmony with the Holy Spirit into being called to serve in the nursery? It is obvious that a piece or two of meaning got lost in the translation.

In Ephesians 4 Paul describes what we would call vocational ministry: apostles, prophets, evangelists, pastors and teachers. He wrote, "walk worthy of the vocation wherewith ye are called" (Ephesians 4:1 KJV). Or walk worthy of the *klēsis* that you are *kaleō*-ed. *Klēsis* is the noun form of *kaleō*. *Klēsis* takes on the meaning of vocation, work, career or circumstance. In other words, it is a way of life and work you find yourself in. Does Paul mean this to be a reference only to how a person serves in spiritual community? Or rather does it refer to living fully into our spiritual nature, our new nature in Christ? One *could* be *kaleō*-ed to offer help to any ministry of the church, the nursery included. But there is still a piece missing, and that piece is passion. Without passion, serial volunteering eventually leaves us feeling left out and discouraged. Certainly there are times when each of us must do the mundane things that make the community run smoothly. We all have to pay our dues. But if that is all we do, there will be trouble in paradise. That cog-in-a-wheel feeling is toxic. It will deflate the souls of the best people, as it did with my friend Theresa. Perhaps if she had found her sweet spot of vocation sooner, she could have endured the monotony of the nursery or the worship team as a part of her service to the Lord. Maybe she would not have burned out.

Common views of calling give way to four myths of *vocatio*: the generic view, the spiritual view, the secular view and the locational view. Let's take a look at these to see if we can find some clarity for this word *calling*.

FOUR MYTHS OF *VOCATIO*

Myth 1: People are called to serve wherever they can find something to do. In the generic view *vocatio* is so nonspecific that it neither endures the test of time nor provides the specificity needed for the unique life experience each of us are meant to have. Theresa responded to a call to serve at her church. In real time, Theresa is a gifted artist and teacher. She can teach the most artistically challenged of us to make beautiful art. Was her call to serve in the nursery a *vocatio* from God or merely a call by the church to participate? In the generic view we do whatever needs to be done without regard to any inner motivation or lack thereof. When we are underutilized, as was the case with Theresa, the most common side effect is boredom. A failure of passion will deflate the souls of the most earnest of people, as it did with Theresa.

Myth 2: A spiritual call comes from the very breath of God. In the spiritual view *vocatio* is thought to come to a person from an outside source, usually God, but it could come from a respected person, such as a parent, a prophet or a pastor. It is subjectively received and immune to verification by those standing on the sidelines, because God said it. Who can argue with that? In fact, he or she may not want to answer the call at all. The person proves his or her deep spirituality by doing it anyway. Often the story of Saul and the blinding light from heaven is used to justify the spiritual view.[8] This view sees Paul's experience as normative rather than the unique and remarkable situation that it was (Acts 9:3-9). The most common aspect of the spiritual view is that the story and history of the one called is not engaged in the discernment process, rather the call comes from outside of the person's experience. Again, Theresa's story is an example of the spiritual view.

Myth 3: Vocation has only to do with your working career. This secular view is the most commonly believed version of vocation.

With this view we merely choose a career, much like students did on career day at my high school, and set a course for the future. The most common element of the secular view is that God's voice is missing. Therefore there is no guidance from the Holy Spirit. It depended on affinity only, meaning what feels right at the time is what is done. It can often be the path of least resistance.

Myth 4: God calls only to specific places and specific people groups. This locational view is self-explanatory and is illustrated by Sue's story. This view left Sue feeling useless when she was no longer able to serve in Africa, where she felt God had called her to serve. A well-developed vocational credo can be exercised almost anywhere at any time. It has longevity and breadth. The most common element of the locational view is lack of breadth and lack of longevity.

Had Sue developed a vocational credo much sooner, she might have been able to appreciate the connection between how she contributed on the mission field and how she might live out her vocation at home. After a process of vocational discernment Sue sought work as a medical advocate for African immigrants, and she loves it as much as she loved her work in Africa. Sue's vocational credo looks something like this: *Sue was put on this earth by God to help Africans become healthier so that they can raise healthy children and build stronger communities.*

> A vocational credo is a carefully crafted statement that describes one's purpose for existence.

The four mythical views each lack a necessary element, whether that be passion, discernment of story, considering the will of God, or longevity and breadth of the call. Vocation happens when heaven and earth kiss. Vocation combines everything that we have experienced, including our pain, our gifts and that which captures our imagination. And then God says, "Why don't you do something about this need? Why don't you use your gifts, your skills and your story? You will be most happy that way!" Who wouldn't want to be part of that adventure?

TOWARD A MORE ACCURATE VIEW OF SELF

Planning the future with an inaccurate view of vocation causes us to default to an inaccurate view of self. When we seek to express vocation in a way that is not meant for us, harm is done to both the one who sacrifices for the sake of others and the folks who would benefit from these efforts. When givers realize that their sacrificial work is unsatisfying, they become resentful. The receiver of their efforts then feels used, realizing that he or she has become a means to make someone else feel good. There is no sweet spot for either. Better to figure out what really needs to happen and do that first! Satisfaction for both giver and receiver is possible when we lead with our own unique gifts.

Although the pathway to a fulfilling vocation was fairly short for Matthew, his story reveals how the four mythical views play out in one story. Matthew's artistic talent was noticeable before he started kindergarten. His high school art teachers predicted grand success in his future as an artist (the spiritual view). Matthew was convinced that his gift would make room for him in the world of graphic arts (locational view), so he attended college and began his career as a graphic artist. Bewildered by his discontent with his career path, he cast about for the right fit (generic view) for a few years without success. Eventually, he rose to the top of the industry, but it was not by using his artistic skills. As it turned out Matthew, the artist, was much better at leadership. He was a people person.

Now Matthew is a successful startup entrepreneur who empowers others to become their best and most powerful selves (the opposite of the secular view) while meeting the needs of community. Matthew the artist became Matthew the CEO. While neither identity is bad in and of itself, Matthew is actualized by his work as a CEO, which makes it a better and more powerful fit. Matthew's vocational credo looks something like this: *God put Matthew on earth to help creative people maximize their potential so they can start businesses that make opportunities for others and meet needs along the way.*

Now that we have established a biblical view of calling and vocation, we will build on these understandings as we begin to discover the importance of your own story in the formation of your vocation.

REFLECTION AND PRACTICE

Reflect on these questions and note your responses.

1. What stands out to you the most from this chapter?

2. Might you have an inaccurate view of your vocation? If so, describe what you are experiencing. If not, describe how you view yourself vocationally.

3. How does your view of self reflect on your values?

4. Where would you like to go from here?

5. Who will walk with you?

How Pain Sets the
Trajectory for Vocation

Although God eventually answered my prayers and gave me three sisters, I grew up predominately in the company of brothers—six of them. Home life was loud and chaotic, and nothing was sacred. In fact, even today I have the reputation of being able to unsettle anyone in the room with my grossology skills learned from my brotherly mentors. If I ever had inclinations toward the finer things in life, the barrel of monkeys in my home dashed those hopes.

My brothers could demolish tangible things in mere seconds. And like the locusts in Egypt they sought and devoured everything in sight. In her frustration my mother developed a commanding response to this abundance of testosterone that threatened to overwhelm us. When pushed to the edge of her boundaries she could yell louder than the whole crew put together. Someday I hoped that I could do the same. But her vocal chords never made it into my gene pool. Unable to compete in the cacophony of my home life, I developed other skills. I learned to work in manipulation like an artist works in oils. Still, I never stopped trying to be heard in the din. This, I am sure, contributed to the hoarse whisper that I was left with.

Other dark events at work in my life contributed to my metaphoric voicelessness. These events would one day converge, pushing me into double silence. My brothers eventually grew into sophisticated and accomplished men, my mother was still her sweet but powerful self, and I became a whisperer, a "low talker." (A low talker was a person portrayed in a *Seinfeld* episode who created social discomfort by barely speaking above a whisper, so she was nearly impossible to understand.) My voice diminished to the point where I could barely be heard; so it appeared as if I was telling people secrets. I felt rude and was socially confusing to others.

Although the *Seinfeld* low talker may not have been based in reality, it was the only description that came close to my pre-diagnosis state. It became impossible to carry on conversations in places that had competing background noise, all the fun places like restaurants, church, parties and even riding in the car.

> The quieter you become, the more you can hear.
>
> RAM DASS[1]

So I lost my job and gave up on most social events. Being an extrovert, and a bossy one at that, I was dying bit by bit as my disability grew. Getting an opinion across, giving input, telling stories or jokes, having an intelligent conversation, these were all sliding off the table for me. In the end, no voice meant limited presence and thus little significance.

LOST VOICE, OPENED EYES

It's interesting what happens when you have to stop talking. Your eyes become opened, painfully opened. Perspective changes. I began noticing a few things that had never caught my attention before. Much like a blind man who develops superhuman hearing to compensate for his lack of sight, I became a keen observer of conversations. And rather than gathering information through words, I began collecting data of the nonverbal variety. I noticed that others had a struggle to be heard too, but it was not so much a literal voice thing. It was something much deeper.

As I became sensitized to the stories beyond words, what they *weren't* saying became more obvious to me than what they *were* saying. There is a multitude of ways that a person can be shut out of a conversation. When one is not invited to the table, his or her point of view does not count. I could hear silent pleas of those who were marginalized: *Let me be more than this!* Yet, they may as well have been voiceless like me because their presence had little effect. In *Faith and Feminism* author Helen LaKelly Hunt writes, "The search for voice is the search for self. The Hebrew God, Yahweh, made the same unassailable statement of beingness: 'I am that I am.'"[2] Voice is each person's unique "I amness."

Voice is our *I amness*. It is essential to fully expressing oneself. Without voice human beings suffer a diminished sense of self and project an incomplete God image, or as LaKelly Hunt would say, an incomplete *I amness*. Everyone loses when that happens because each human being has a unique contribution to the world that only he or she can bring.

> Nobody can be exactly like me. Sometimes even I have trouble doing it.
>
> TALLULAH BANKHEAD

Voice became my obsession. I sensed that God was presenting me with a gift, a metaphor that would change my life, but I didn't understand it, not yet anyway.

All I knew was that my voicelessness had betrayed me because

I could not express myself. Hopes, dreams and opportunities were flying away like the snow geese who take to the wing to find a more hospitable wintering ground. My future was slipping away into oblivion. Then hope arrived, sort of. I found a clinic that would treat my condition with the best medicine available.

Every six months the doctor would give me shots directly into my throat, which caused me to choke. Swallowing was nearly impossible for days afterward. It was a month before I could talk out loud, and that only lasted for a few months. Then the whole routine started all over again. I was wearied by these ghoulish medical treatments that promised results but only partially delivered.

Somewhere along the way, though, my focus began to shift from literal voice to voice as a symbolic expression of passion and meaning. The idea of a voice beyond words stirred my imagination. It was a way to assign meaning to myself and what I was experiencing, as well as to other voiceless people that I had come to know. I wanted more than anything to heal myself and hoped that in the process I could help heal others. I earnestly sought answers. Even though the answers I had hoped for didn't arrive quickly, I kept pushing my way forward one step at a time. Those steps began to turn into a pathway, for me first and then eventually for the others that I wanted so earnestly to help.

EMBRACING THE BROKENNESS

My desire to be significant overwhelmed my disability, and I became determined to fight my way out of my dark, little corner. I was tired of being alone and decided that I was not willing to abandon a fruitful, active future to a mundane and silent existence. Imagination is a powerful tool. I felt a glimmer of hope that I might be able to communicate in other ways. I developed new ways to work without a voice so I could again start dreaming about the future. I was able to go back to work. Passion, I discovered, could function jolly well without the aid of words.

Quite by accident I stumbled upon a specialist who had a different approach to healing. He helped me to recover a fragile but functioning voice. I was thrilled about the world that was opening once again to me. It would have been natural to walk away from the voice issue right then and go back to life how it was. But I could not. My heart had been captured. My fascination with voice was now coloring how I was seeing my world. The imaginings of gaining a powerful voice, both kinds, was by the day acquiring real estate in my soul. My hope was returning. I sensed more than ever that I was on a God journey.

Helen LaKelly Hunt says that we "voice ourselves into existence." Oddly, voicelessness had called me out in a proactive way. It was voicing me into a life-consuming endeavor. Not only did I desire voice for myself, but I felt compelled to fight for it for others. I wanted to become a liberator of the expression and purpose of my silent friends. It is no coincidence that helping others find their voice, and vocation as an extension of that voice, is what drives me today and probably will for the rest of my life. This calling, my vocation, was a result of the trajectory of my struggle with hardship and loss. I finally realized that this was the gift that God had hidden for me in my pain and loss.

Like a child who dreams of flying
And aches for something more
We hold the dim remembrance
Of an ancient golden shore
Ah, but now our faith is frozen
We lost it by default
I tell you if we linger
We will all be turned to salt

Come where the Big Wind blows
Out on the wild frontier
Follow where it goes
Out on the wild frontier
It's as close as your heartbeat
It's as far as your fear
It's beyond the great horizon
Out on the wild frontier[3]

These lyrics were written by singer Randy Stonehill. The song speaks of the challenge of leaving a safe but dull place and rushing headlong into the wild unknown to find the promised land. I did not appreciate his message in this song until I found the courage to embrace my pain and loss. I sensed that I needed to run to the wild frontier and beyond it to find my own promised land. I began to understand the thrill of the ride. Today I can hardly hear this song without experiencing an adrenaline rush. I want this experience to recur over and over again in my life because the wild frontier is where I sense God working the strongest.

> It's as close as your heartbeat.
> It's as far as your fear.
> RANDY STONEHILL

In the exploration of the American West the pioneer never knew what lay around the next bend. There were no road signs to mark the way, no well-worn paths, no assurances of food or water or safety. It was wild indeed! Fear was dichotomous, both a life-preserving companion as well as being antithetical to new discoveries. Knowing when to respect the fear and when to blast through it required wisdom. This is not unlike the vocational journey today. This change that God asks of us is daunting, and we do not know exactly what the outcome will be. The best we can do is give ourselves to the process, trusting that the Holy Spirit will lead us to challenges of growth and transformation while leading us away from that which would harm us and those around us.

While I have a personality that welcomes the adventures of the wild frontier, I recognize that many others may not enjoy the surprises and challenges of the unknown. I can imagine that among the pioneers who settled the West there were those who only went on this adventure because it was necessary for their survival. Some may have tagged along with others who had a greater taste for adventure. These people took the long and arduous journey to their promised land one day at a time. Some turned back. Many left most of their possessions behind. But the unknown was less of a threat to their existence than staying in their quiet lives of desperation.

How might the challenges of the wild frontier work transformation in us? How does change find its way from the mind to the heart and then to our actions? How does a life become something other than what it was? These are very important questions if we are serious about becoming the best possible version of ourselves. It is possible to spend an entire lifetime hoping and even praying for change while never experiencing it because of a broken idea of how change works.

Because there is no way to know what lies on the other side, change can be a frightening process. Few are comfortable with this level of the unknown. And to add to the angst, transformational change is an extremely high-risk proposition because it is absolutely irreversible. Just like the butterfly who can never return to the cocoon for safety and comfort, we are offered no return to former circumstances once transformation has occurred. In the movie *The Matrix*, Morpheus challenges Neo, "This is your last chance. After this, there is no turning back. You take the blue pill—the story ends, you wake up in your bed and believe whatever you want to believe. You take the red pill—you stay in Wonderland and I show you how deep the rabbit-hole goes."[4]

Once the red pill had been swallowed there was no going back to a blissful state of ignorance, of not acknowledging the truth of the matrix. The blue pill continued the ignorance as well as a pacified and contented existence. The red pill brought reality, a visceral reality along with the thrill of life on the edge of the wild frontier in a life or death game. These are the choices available to us as well. Like the pioneers in *The Matrix*, all who decided they wanted change, we must wrestle with this question, How far down the rabbit hole am I willing to go?

The risk that Stonehill sings about in "Wild Frontier" describes chaotic disruption. It demands a willingness to journey into the darkest fear. Only God knows how deep the rabbit hole will go for any of us. I didn't find change without a crisis. I was compelled to move forward into unknown territory to find healing and significance rather than choosing slow death in my small, quiet world. In all of my pain, and in the challenge of building a new way to live, chaos became beautiful.

> We could never learn to be brave and patient if there were only joy in the world.
> HELEN KELLER[5]

The obvious point here is that transformation comes neither from times of great joy and safety nor well-orated lectures, sermons or the latest self-help books. Rather, risk and loss bring transformational change. Transformation finds fertile territory when risk and loss are embraced. As the saying goes, "Pain is inevitable. Suffering is optional." Each one of us has to choose whether we will allow pain to do its good work. If we do not allow it, then suffering reigns.

If pain is acknowledged and allowed to teach us, it will become our mentor. Pain is rescued from suffering and brought to significance through the discovery of meaning. Pain that has meaning is called productive pain. Of course there is unproductive pain such as childhood cancer or pain as a result of evil actions. But in stark contrast to unproductive pain, productive pain does a good work in the life of the sufferer. Any woman who has ever given birth understands this. At the end of her pain she holds newborn life in her arms. Productive pain leaves us with something that we can hold onto, an end product, whether a baby, deeper faith, more confidence in oneself or some other kind of new life or hope. When we believe in the product, we have the ability to endure the process.

> We cannot learn without pain.
> ARISTOTLE

Productive pain is pain with meaning. Meaning underlays the development of passion. Meaning produces a volcano of fire within our souls that causes us to overflow the bounds of the ordinary. This is passion. Passion is described as sustained energy that has staying power. Passion that is focused and practically lived out for the benefit of others is called a vocation. Here is a simple graphic to help you remember the progression:

Pain → Meaning → Passion → Vocation

Figure 3.1

REFLECTION AND PRACTICE

Ponder these questions and note your responses:

1. What could be the wild frontier for you?

2. When have you swallowed the red pill? What about the blue pill?

3. What lessons did you learn about yourself?

4. How have those lessons inspired you?

Illumination from Darkness

The loss of my voice scarred me deeply. As I embrace my story I see that my literal loss of voice was not the only event that contributed to my voicelessness. Though unintentionally, the overwhelming troop of brothers in my home drowned me out. As a young child I was sexually abused by a man who silenced me by threatening harm to my family. This devastated my young soul. The church that I grew up in had no grid for female vocational strength in ministry. In seminary it was communicated, in no uncertain terms, that women had neither ability nor calling from God to lead in substantive ways. These events crushed my soul a bit more with each blow, creating a numbness that clung to me like a tar baby. It was a negative prophecy over my life that was seeking to destroy me and rob abundance from my future. These unfortunate events, along with the weakness of my speaking voice, culminated in the loss of voice on multiple levels.

I silently shouted to God to show me what purpose, if any, could spring from my story. I longed to work with my story rather than in spite of it. After journeying through the darkest of nights, it began to dawn on me that what these negative events had done to my soul was not intended to be fatal. Instead they were meant to create a powerful pushback.

I soon began developing a working relationship with my dilemma that looked like this: At first I tried to ignore my fading voice. Next it was something that I bore. Then I hated my weakness. After a while I figured out how to get around my disability. And, finally, I embraced my voicelessness as a gift from God. Part of that gift was anger. I raged against voicelessness. *No more!* was my internal mantra. I vowed that I would no longer be silent. Coincidentally, about that same time I began studying Hebrew. I discovered that my name, Deborah, comes from a Hebrew word, *dabar*, which means "to speak" or "give voice to." My brain and my heart exploded simultaneously. Even my name was prophesying my future. My voice issue had come full circle. I now felt the comfort of God that comes from knowing I was exactly where I was supposed to be. God had the redemption of my story in mind from the very day I was named.

It occurred to me that I, as a broken woman, spent so much time and effort hiding my scars when the world wanted a little honesty from me. People wanted to know how I hung on to God and my spirituality in spite of my pain and loss. Rather than perfection, living from my brokenness would be sustainable and rich with possibilities that would pull me forward into my future.

Next we will look at the story of Esther. She also is a woman who found her way forward in spite of even greater odds.

FOR SUCH A TIME AS THIS

In Esther's time the Jews were exiles in Persia. They had been conquered and carried away by the Babylonians and ended up in the city of Susa. The Persian king Xerxes gave the Jews the opportunity to return to Jerusalem, but many did not go. Esther's family and friends were among those who chose to stay. As the story goes, Esther was responsible for saving her entire nation at the peril of her own life. After this event we don't hear any more about her. Establishing safety and salvation for the Jewish nation was her piece to play in history. The question is, how did she get there? Why was she so willing to risk her life for her people? Where did her well of strength come from?

Some said that she was a descendant of royalty, Kish, one of Israel's previous kings. That would have made Esther's plight all the more extreme. Why would a girl of royal blood be found living off the kindness of others? Esther, whose name means "star," must have wondered how she would ever make something of herself. She was on the bottom looking up, a far cry from the stars in the heavens.

The Bible says that Esther was beautiful. If she was a normal young woman, she would have had male admirers; maybe she had a love interest with whom she was planning a future. Friends and an active social life would have been the norm. Since the prophets instructed the Jews to live the same way they lived before exile, her life must have been unremarkable in any outwardly discernible way, that is until we are invited into her story (see the Old Testament book of Esther). Although the text does not give us any clues about this, I wonder if her friends saw evidence of her boldness or her penchant for risk taking. Did her cousin Mordecai, who raised Esther, notice her focus and her cool restraint as she went about her daily life? These qualities and more were simmering inside of Esther, probably mostly unnoticed, that is until that day, the day of the beauty call.

Esther was swept up in a collection of the most beautiful women of the land. The situation was probably out of the control of either Esther or Mordecai. However, I wonder why the duo did not resist a scheme that was so blatantly forbidden by Jewish laws. Fathers were forbidden to give their virgin daughters to non-Jewish men, not to mention the social implications of life in a harem. These looming details seemed to escape both Mordecai and Esther, suggesting that there was something much larger at work in their story. Although Mordecai could have hidden Esther, he did not. What normally would have stuck in the craw of a Jew didn't seem to faze Mordecai or Esther.

Once inside the palace, Esther would compete against the most beautiful women from all ethnicities and cultures from every Persian province.[1] No doubt, she had some stiff competition. If Esther did not win the contest, there would be no husband, possibly no children, certainly no life as it would have been. The risk was profound and the odds were stacked against her. In the unlikely event that she managed to escape the harem, postharem life would be fraught with danger and rejection. She would be damaged goods to the men of her tribe and a byword among her people. Yet something primal inside of Esther caused her to lunge toward this challenge rather than to shrink from it. Based on the outcomes of her story, we can make some guesses why. It is certainly possible—but not probable—that Esther grew up oblivious to the facts of her existence. More realistically she was unable to forget her position in the family and the community.

From the very beginning Esther faced three seemingly insurmountable obstacles. First, she was female in a patriarchal society where very few options existed outside of the prescribed female roles. Being an orphan was strike two. She was called the daughter of Abihail, not the daughter of Mordecai. Although Mordecai loved her and raised her as his own, the child Esther would have wondered why her parents had to die. She knew she was an orphan. And third, she was living as a Hebrew exile in a foreign land, with odd customs and strange languages.

Realistically, Esther could not forget the circumstances that limited her future. It is probable that her plight evoked an inner argument that sounded a bit like this, *Someday I will be a star. I will rise to greatness.* The outcomes of her story demanded that Esther strongly push back against her circumstances. That resistance created in her the boldness to step forward one day and say, "Choose me!" And on yet another day she would cry out, "No more!" for the sake of her people.

THE RISING STAR

As the scriptural story of Esther unfolds, it becomes immediately obvious that she would accept victory and no less. Along with the other girls that entered the palace, Esther was given one year of beauty treatments. These were meant to work the roughness out of those who had been rounded up in the beauty call. They were trained in the ways of social graces, extravagance and sensuality. How odd this must have been for Esther, an orphan girl from a religious culture.

The next time we see the pre-queen she is preparing herself for a night with the king. She is strategic in her requests and requires only what the keeper of the harem recommends. She wisely trusts him as a mentor, proving that she is no fool. She pleases the king more than any other and Xerxes crowns her as his queen.

It is not long, however, before Esther's mettle is tested in a different way. Mordecai's conflict with Haman, a rival in the king's court, quickly escalates into a life or death dilemma for Esther. Putting her life in jeopardy, she approaches the king unbidden, which carried a potential death sentence. Much to her relief, he warmly receives her, and through some great drama she reveals Haman's plot to destroy the Jews.

By now the king has offered her half his kingdom, not once or twice but three times. In Hebrew storytelling, repetition is an indicator of importance by emphasis. The king loved her so much that he offered her equality of ownership, which was very rare, and a point that the author does not want the reader to miss. How much did the king love Esther? He loved her a lot—times three. There was not a doubt where the king's loyalty rested.

If Esther had been in it for herself, she could have cut a deal with the king and saved her own skin. Esther exhibited all-or-nothing solidarity with her people. And with great restraint she successfully bargained for the lives of the Jews, who were scattered about the Persian provinces. Their enemy, the anti-Semitic Haman, was sent to the gallows, and Esther's people were given the right to fight back. The Jewish holiday of Purim celebrates her victory.[2]

Esther did not get into the palace by accident. The painful events of her short story drew her forward into a destiny that was ordained by God to liberate her people. No one knew what strategic events would play out within her reach, but God did. By the time she was presented with the opportunity to save her people, Esther was so prepared for her mission that she didn't need much time to think about it. She merely acted.

ONCE UPON A TIME

What makes a great story, author Kathryn Schulz says, "is when you think one thing is going to happen and then something else happens instead."[3] In a well-constructed story the plot twists and turns give the players in the story the opportunity to show themselves, their character strengths and weaknesses, which in turn provide rich fodder for surprises, humor and life lessons. We all love a good story, especially one that inspires us.

The Bible is rife with stories that surprise and inspire, stories of the oppressed, the broken and the sick who have overcome great odds to do epic things. In fact, nearly every story in the Bible follows a trajectory of a life that moves from pain, oppression or loss to a great risk and then an ending of legendary proportions.

The people in these stories show us how the ordinary can become extraordinary. Normal, everyday people become superstars: an old man builds a massive boat to save his family and a multitude of animals from the water falling from the sky; a woman far too old to bear children gets pregnant and births a nation; a man is told to murder his son, and a ram appears out of nowhere, saving his son and the nation in his loins; a murderer becomes the deliverer of an enslaved people; a boy kills a lion and then a giant; another boy escapes the lion's den; three young Hebrews emerge unscathed from a fiery furnace; a woman drives a tent peg through the enemy king's head; another woman leads her country in battle to an unlikely victory; a thresher of wheat becomes a mighty warrior; and so the stories go.

These stories help us get in touch with our inner heroes. They inspire us to want to be more than we are, and urge us to discover our own stories. And when we discover our own stories, they help us to find purpose in them.

CUSTODIANS OF MEMORY

Writer William Zinsser said, "Writers are the custodians of memory, and that's what you must become if you want to leave some kind of record of your life and of the family you were born into."[4] This is what the writers of the Bible have done for us. They have been the custodians of our God memory.

Zinsser makes a salient point for those who wish to make their impression on the world. Although we are not all writers, we are the keepers of our own stories. You may not think you have a story worth telling, yet it is surprising how weighty your story might be. I am guessing that many of our Bible characters did not think their stories were worth telling either.

Is there room for the ordinary? I have a friend whose name is Blue Mike. Blue Mike stands on the most populated street corner in downtown Portland. Mike says he is called to maintain "the peace and tranquility of this corner." So he is downtown nearly every day greeting people as they pass by, bringing a smile to many faces. I must mention that he paints himself blue, his face, his hair, his hands, anything visible. And he wears a blue hoodie. Mike is a dear man who does what he knows God has called him to do. And if you knew him, you would know that God called him to do it too. Mike is the custodian of his own story. He knows who he is and what he is all about. He has a simple and beautiful calling that, although unusual, is not spectacular.

I have another friend named Jane. She was widowed a few years ago and her new self has come out to play in a fun way since then. Although she spent most of her life married to Tony, a larger-than-life minister, Jane had and always will have deep, probing questions that provoke thought about life, death, humanity and God. Her vocational credo might be to bring people to understand the true character of God through thought and conversation.

Maybe you weren't born to heal malaria on the continent of Africa like Bill and Melinda Gates, or to discover the cure for leukemia, or how to sustain life on the moon. Your story is still very important, and it might be as simple as Mike's or Jane's. Recall Frankl's words from chapter one:

> Everyone has his own specific vocation or mission in life: everyone must carry out a concrete assignment that demands fulfillment. Therein he cannot be replaced, nor can his life be repeated, thus everyone's task is unique as is his specific opportunity to implement it.[5]

Nobody can do what you do. We are meant to become heroes in our own stories in a way that is most natural for us. The Bible has something to say about how this might work on an elementary yet profound level, and it has to do with empathy.

COMFORT AND CALLING

> Praise be to the God and Father of our Lord Jesus Christ, the Father of compassion and the God of all *comfort*, who *comforts* us in all our troubles, so that we can *comfort* those in any trouble with the *comfort* we ourselves receive from God. For just as we share abundantly in the sufferings of Christ, so also our *comfort* abounds through Christ. (2 Corinthians 1:3-5, emphasis added)

Remember that when a word is used more than once in a Scripture, it is meant to make us stop and think. *Comfort* comes up five times in this passage. This is *comfort* on steroids! The writer wants us to know just how important this act of comfort is. The words used for comfort in the Greek are from the same family of words used for vocation and calling, except they include the prefix *para*: *parakaleō* and *paraklēsis*. This prefix gives these words the meaning of "called alongside."[6] We are called alongside of suffering to bring comfort in the way we ourselves have been comforted. It means that experiences of pain are not wasted but are the lifelong building blocks for vocation.

Rather than sink us into bitterness, pain is meant to develop empathy in the soul if we choose to pay attention to it. The Holy Spirit is embodied in me when I actively empathize. The sufferer relaxes into God's very presence while in my arms. *My* comfort must preclude my attempts at comfort or I am offering something with which I have no experience. My experience is key to the process. Therefore, as the comforter I must learn how to tell my story of comfort, the story that caused empathy to grow in me. I can only do that through brave explorations of my past wounds.

In 1996 researcher Giacomo Rizzolatti discovered "mirror neurons" in human beings and in other primates. These mirror neurons are also called "empathy neurons." What is most striking, says Rizzolatti, is that "mirror neurons allow us to grasp the minds of others not through conceptual reasoning but through direct stimulation. By feeling, not by thinking."[7] Scientists can prove the dynamics of empathy scientifically. It should come as no surprise that we are hardwired to empathize. In fact, it makes 2 Corinthians 1:3-5 all the more meaningful.

My vocation emerged from the themes of pain as well as the comfort I experienced in the arms of those who became *paraklētos* to me. I love those who are voiceless and unheard, however this came about in their lives. I seek to comfort them by helping them know that they have a right to their own voice. I want others to be free to tell their own truth. *That* is what brings me my deepest joy. Knowing our own story of pain and comfort, and being able to tell it is absolutely key to comfort and therefore to vocation.

Finding your story requires a hard look into hidden and protected corners of personal history. This is your wild frontier. The dark themes of our lives have the potential to lead us to significance and meaning, but it is most often terrifying and therefore risky territory to explore. Vocation is the reward to that risk. Many folks struggle to find significance even though they want it badly. If this is you, you will be excited about this good news: although it is impossible to prophesy the future, it is possible to discern what the future might hold for you through thoughtful examination of the events of your life. Nobody says it better than Dan Allender in his book *To Be Told*:

The future is meant to be written in light of the patterns of the past. We can't predict the future, but we can read the patterns of the past to see how God has marked us for his purposes. He uses the past to open our future. As we learn to read patterns, we gain an understanding of our calling.[8]

Vocation, which Allender refers to as "calling," is the redeemed outcomes of those patterns. In my story and in Esther's, the redeemed outcomes are easy to see. The hard work has been done for you and laid out neatly on the page. However, it is not so easy to discover your own patterns. I will do my best to help you along in your exploration.

Are you ready to discover your own personal wild frontier? The best place to start looking for your patterns is by examining your seasons of pain. Although I am no therapist or counselor, years of life on this planet have presented me with a few observations about myself and others.

I have observed that first pains usually cause long-lasting emotional impressions. They are rude awakenings at a very young age that attest to the fact that the world is not always a kind place. Few people forget them. In fact when other painful situations occur, we connect them to the pain that we already know and draw conclusions about our inherent worth from them. As you might guess, most of those conclusions are not positive. These negative self-thoughts forge a well-trodden pathway of pain within us. We keep it hidden in the darkness in order to protect ourselves. Once uncovered, our pathways of pain are the seeds of our best stories. We need these stories in order to discover our *why*, our *how* and our *what*. We will get to the *how* and the *what* in later chapters. Let's work on your *why* first.

In the introduction I mentioned that my first major experience of pain occurred at the hands of a male abuser when I was quite young. That wound was reopened by abusive boyfriends and acquaintances, culminating in date rape, each with increasing pain and negative conclusions about my worth. It seemed as though I had a sign on my back, readable only to abusers, that said, "Use me. I won't tell."

Because I felt a deep sense of shame as a result of the abuse, I convinced myself that my story was not important enough to tell. At the time I did not go to therapy or to the police. I knew that if I risked uncovering my shame, my life would become unbearable. So I did not tell anyone. I accepted fear and shame as lifelong companions. As I collected pain experiences from other disappointments and abuses, I tossed them onto the hidden pain pile that became a mountainous heap of rejection, marginalization, fear and oppression. I felt snuffed out, and out of discouragement I gave up. This led to a season in my life of addiction and self-destruction. In reality I became voiceless long before I physically lost my voice.

REFLECTION AND PRACTICE

Dan Allender says, "Whatever has broken our heart is meant to arouse our anger."[9] What is making you angry? How would you like to voice your anger? Like Esther, what are you saying "no more" to? Take a moment to consider your own story. What is the first wounding experience—physical, emotional or otherwise—you remember? Don't think too hard about this; it should come unbidden. This exercise will help you.

1. Draw a simple representation of your life on a piece of paper. This could be a line or a forest or a representation of your physical body. Use your imagination.

2. Place your first wound anywhere that seems appropriate on

your image. Note the emotions you were feeling. If you can say "I felt _____," it is probably an emotion. If you say, "I felt like_____," you are creating a metaphor for the pain. Getting to the emotion behind the metaphor is important because it leads to your passion.

3. Indicate other times that you experienced this pain. Are there any recurring emotional themes or negative experiences that connect with your first wound? Note them.

4. You will be using the vocational triangle (see. fig. 4.1) to build visual connections between a few bits of information that will help you to discover your passion and thus your vocation.[10] Write your first wound in one or two words on the far left point of the triangle.

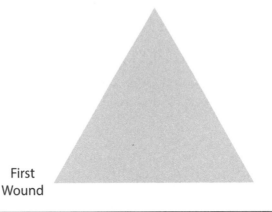

First
Wound

Figure 4.1. The vocational triangle

5

The Puzzle Pieces of Your Story

S ometimes people ask me to speak at their organization's events, and I love doing this. I have spoken at a wide variety of venues, including churches, classrooms, conferences, workshops and businesses, and they always want me to tell a little bit about myself as an introduction. I am typically asked to describe my education and work accomplishments. I am not very excited about that conversation. I would rather talk about what inspires me, which happens to be the future rather than the past.

So I say something like this, "I can tell you about my accomplishments, my degrees, my jobs and my travels. They are certainly foundational to who I am in many ways. But I would rather discuss what inspires me, that which has formed me into who I am today. I am inspired by voice. It is my passion. The reason I am here, the reason God created me, is to help others find their voice and vocation so they can serve God and community with greater creativity and power, and change the world. I want us all to work together to change the world!"

It does not matter what I have been asked to talk about, I usually start with that short speech. Here is why: Which is more compelling: my statistics or my passion? Which makes you more curious? Which description of myself helps you to understand me more quickly and intimately? Which pushes toward the future? Passion is contagious. Everyone wants to be inspired. My desire is to pull folks into their futures by discovering and understanding their own passions. Which description of myself does that better?

Knowing your passion is a powerful bit of self-knowledge. I look for any chance to talk about my passion, because that is what inspires others to find their own voice. My little speech is on my résumé, and it is usually one of the first things that I say about myself when interviewing for a speaking engagement or project. Everyone should be able to present him- or herself with this kind of strong self-knowledge. Doing so creates pathways of opportunity and influence, and it creates the future. Your thoughtfully constructed vocational credo will open doors for *you*. My goal is to bring you one step closer to your credo through a few more counterintuitive exercises. Hang in there, it will be fun!

YOU ARE A WHAT?

As I ascended the stairs to the podium, the worship leader and the musicians, all college students, were leaving the stage. Spirit still lingering in the air, it was obvious that we were standing on holy ground. As the guest speaker at this undergraduate university, I was supposed to tell about myself, but it just didn't seem appropriate. With a pause, I looked around the two-thousand-plus students in the auditorium. Pointing to their leader I said, "This man is not a worship leader."

A hushed gasp wafted through the auditorium, and then the room became pin-drop silent. They were afraid of what I might say next. I looked around the auditorium once again and said, "This man is a curator who brings human beings face to face with the

God of the universe." I continued, "And *that*, folks, is a far greater calling than that of a worship leader. That is a vocation." Sighs of relief exhaled all over the auditorium. The controversy that they feared did not materialize. But they understood what I meant, because they too had just experienced this man's vocation.

Too often skills, tools and talents are mistaken for vocation. Music was this college man's tool. His passion was something much deeper. As he led the crowd in worship, I noticed that he turned an ear toward heaven and then toward the students, all while guiding the orchestra in swells of beautiful melody punctuated with silent anticipation. Worship leader, musician and singer are all aspects or tools of his vocation, but they are not his vocation. He facilitates space and atmosphere where relationships between God and people can blossom and grow. There is an appreciable difference.

I live in Portland, Oregon. Musicians, sculptors, painters, dancers and actors flock here in droves. This is, after all, the place where young people come to retire.[1] Somebody is always recording, going on tour, preparing an installation or getting ready for opening night. These supertalented young people soon learn that there is very little room at the top of the fame heap. As a result many are unemployed or work coffee. It is difficult to live on barista wages, so they live five or more to a house.

Portland's young creatives need to know that there is hope for them to be actualized, that is, to find work that utilizes their skills *and* their passions. But who helps them know that there is significance that runs deeper than merely their talents? If these amazing folks do not find a way forward, they will run out of gas and linger by the roadside for who knows how long. They will lose hope, stumble and fall. Sarah is one of those people. A look at her story will illustrate how the work of finding vocation could bring greater significance to a generation of artists.

Sarah tried to convince me that performing was her vocation. "I am a thespian. I have never felt as actualized as I do when I am on stage!" she exhaled in breathy melodrama. I suggested that she may have her ego confused with her vocation. She did not think I was funny. I was trying to make a point as well as offer much-needed comedic relief. Sarah was a young and gifted actress who had worked at her craft since she was a teenager. But a vocation it was not. She was particularly self-consumed. Although Sarah was a great storyteller, she had not incorporated vision or empathy for others in her performances. The majority of her creativity was self-oriented and narcissistic.

Through my workshop Sarah began to get in touch with her pain, the stuff that had deeply shaped her life. She soon discovered that she possessed a powerful ability to enact her own story while reaching out to others who have suffered in the same way she did. Often people were moved to tears by her performances. Eventually she developed a mission to help heal others through dramatic vignettes.

Sarah created a company that addressed generative themes in short story form inspired by the angst of her teen years.[2] Sarah's vocation was that of a communicator and healer, much more powerful than merely an actor. Her vocational credo looked something like this: *Sarah is on this earth to heal others emotionally and spiritually through her gift of storytelling.* After a few years Sarah's life circumstances changed and she could no longer work as an actress, but she found new ways to heal people by teaching them to tell their own stories.

So how do you know whether what you do is your vocation? If you describe yourself by saying, "*I am a* _____," you are talking about your learned skills and natural talents, or you are naming a job title rather than a vocation. However if you can say, "I am on this earth to _____" or "My passion is _____" you are probably describing a vocation. Table 5.1 provides some examples of jobs and vocations for the same activities.

Table 5.1. Examples of jobs and vocations

Job Title *I am a(n)*	Vocation *My passion is*
Elementary school teacher	curating environments for children that inspire their imaginations and curiosity
Engineer	solving problems by tackling tough issues that stump others
Physical therapist	helping people to adjust to a healthier lifestyle so they can live longer and be a blessing to others
Lawyer	teaching equality, justice and reverence for others that promotes greater love and peace in the city
Pastor	establishing communities of hope, comfort and challenge so that all might thrive and feel loved
Pastor's spouse	curating spaces that facilitate spirituality, comfort and challenge so that people can grow into service to God and each other
Author	telling the truth that allows people to live freely outside the box
Cab driver	facilitating moments of hospitality and warmth while helping people to get where they need to go
Event planner	creating pleasant experiences where people can relax and make new friends while enjoying old friends

Notice that each of the credos in table 5.1 contains an *active* verb: *curate, solve, help, teach, establish, tell, facilitate, create.* Your verb guides your expression of vocation. Notice that vocation works at a much deeper level than a job title can possibly describe. It also has a much broader application, meaning that the vocational description that each of these persons wrote could be used in different settings. While not discounting the job skills, tools and talents entirely, notice how, in contrast, vocation draws out a person's heart motivation.

POWER BY ASSOCIATION

I would like to digress for a moment to discuss power by association. Power by association happens when people with little self-value use their relationship with a stronger or more well-known person to give them significance. Although this happens in a variety of relationships, the most common setting is marriage. When someone marries a person who needs excessive support from the home front to do a job or to get training, the other spouse often abandons his or her own career in favor of supporting the spouse. Men have traditionally made more money in the marketplace, but there are some preliminary indicators that this is changing. While at one time having the wife support her husband as a homemaker made perfect sense, it does less so today. Women have found their way into the job market with no signs of retreat. It is time to think differently about who does what. Why shouldn't both spouses enjoy opportunities to grow outside of traditional roles?

Seasons do come along in life that require supporting a spouse in some way. Some couples take turns supporting each other so that they both can become actualized in their own chosen vocational pathway. When I signed up for seminary, my husband supported me by cooking, doing laundry, running errands and earning most of the money to pay the bills. A few years after I finished my degrees, he decided to further his education. Our roles were then reversed, and I cooked, cleaned and earned the paycheck. When neither of us no longer needed support in that way, we each returned to our own pursuits and shared household duties and finances equally. However, too often the supportive spouse never gets back in the game. This tendency toward rigid roles is never more common than in religious occupations. Many ministry couples plan on this dynamic as a long-term lifestyle.

I will never forget the first time a woman told me that she was going to Bible college for her MRS degree.[3] I had never heard of that concentration. What could it be? She explained that she was looking to marry a man who aspired to be a pastor. As it turned out the MRS degree was, in fact, a MR focus. She and her friends chose their college according to the percentage of men who became pastors after graduation. These women aspired to be pastors' wives as if it were a job.

I would like to suggest that rather than a vocation, *wife* is a description of how one relates to a husband. Maybe these women believed that this pathway to ministry was the only viable choice for them. I am saddened that this has been their experience. There are so many things wrong with this plan that it's impossible to begin to address them in this book.

Just to set the record straight, I spent five years as a pastor's wife. This is not an easy way to live. Both the woman and her children live in a glass house. Very often churches rely on two for the price of one, so the woman works without her name showing up on a paycheck. Suffice it to say, in most cases the dynamic is unhealthy because the wife gives up her personal power in an unhealthy way. I have sat with many of these women in their later years, some now alone, to help them discern vocation. Many of them have expressed deep regret over lost opportunity and what they perceive to be lost time. The good news is that it is never too late.

In *Real Power*, author Janet Hagberg describes six levels of empowerment.[4] Level one is called "Powerlessness." At level one, a person is without self-determination. In fact they believe that external forces alone control their destiny. They are not authentically themselves. Examples of this would be drug addicts, alcoholics, abused women, people trapped in hierarchical paradigms and all those who believe they do not have a choice about what happens to them. By contrast level six, the highest level, is called "The Sage."[5] The sage has internalized power through spiritual practice and life experience. We all know a few sages. They seem to engage an inner well of wisdom and thought unknown to the rest of us. Sages have an irrepressible sense of well-being and connectedness to the world, and they do not fear death.

With those two extremes in mind, let's look at stage two, which is called "Power by Association." It describes people who are important not in and of themselves but because of the reputation or presence of another. Power at this stage comes from outside of a person. The locus of power is in the important person with whom the person is associated. A good example of this is Jim the name-dropper. Jim is important because of who he knows. Rather than discovering his own value, he tells his friends, acquaintances and associates about the important people he knows. And that is what makes him feel important inside.

Another example of power by association is Letti, a wife of a larger-than-life personality. She does not develop a personal identity beyond that of her famous, or rather infamous, spouse. Rather than dreaming her own dreams, Letti carries his. And she has clout because of his influence. She rarely attempts to explore her own vocational potential because she is convinced that she does not have to. The MRS women fit this profile. Importance and power in the church will come to them by association.

In the movie *The Lord of the Rings* Frodo is tasked to return a ring that has destructive and evil powers.[6] Once returned to its origin, the ring's power would be nullified. Frodo was uniquely gifted to carry the ring, which had the power to utterly destroy his friend Samwise or anyone else who touched it. Samwise's earlier encounter with the ring had convinced him that he was no match for its seductive powers. Samwise vowed to accompany Frodo on this hero's mission. In his fight to return the ring, Frodo eventually exhausted himself so deeply that he lost all touch with his former existence and barely clung to life. In an act of sheer desperation Samwise declares, "I can't carry it [the ring] for you, but I can carry you. Come on!" Samwise then heads up the mountainside with his friend slung over his shoulder. Frodo and Samwise needed each other for a successful mission. Each Hobbit did what he was meant to do.

Nobody is able to carry your ring. You must carry the responsibility of fulfilling your own vocation yourself. You may have a Samwise in your life who would agree to carry you, but this should never be a long-term arrangement. No one gets a free pass to significance or a future. Even if you are related to someone who is ridiculously famous, extremely clever or funny, or blindingly good looking, the power that you obtain from this person is not fair to either of you. You cannot ask this person to carry the significance that your life is intended to have because, like Samwise, Frodo and the ring, it cannot nor should it be done for you.

If this is you, if you have formed your life around a larger-than-life leader, whether a pastor, a high-level executive or a celebrity, do not despair. This book gives you a way to your own significance. It is not too late. Engage in the process laid out on these pages. You will not regret it. As you discover your value, develop your dreams and carry them to fulfillment yourself, you will accomplish your mission. Is it easy? Probably not. But it will be worth it for you and those whose lives you will touch.

STORIES THAT SHAPE YOU

I grew up reading a book called *Harold and the Purple Crayon*.[7] It's about a little boy in foot pajamas with a huge purple crayon. With this crayon he could create any reality he wanted. Sometimes his own imagination carried him away and he found himself in frightful situations. But no problem, he merely drew another scenario and walked out of the scary story and into a safer one. He drew himself into uncharted territory a few times, but he always ended up back at home in his cozy little bed.

I eventually outgrew the elementary reading level that *Harold and the Purple Crayon* offered, but Harold's story remained with me until I was well into my teen years. I was captivated by little Harold's courage and creativity. When my own children were small I introduced them to Harold, and they learned to love him almost as much as I did. Now, many years later, a copy of *Harold and the Purple Crayon* sits on the bookshelf in my office.

My favorite story reveals a lot about me. I have a high value for creativity, courage and adventure. I believe that people have a choice in almost any situation. I also believe that the God who created the world and gave us Jesus as the pathway to salvation will provide us with creative ways to solve any kind of problem. And I also think that the world, in general, is a good place, and that we can expect goodness from the hand of the Creator. There is nothing so fearsome that it cannot be conquered with a little creativity. Even if I get carried away, God and I will rewrite the script and get me back on track.

I am not alone in my thoughts about the effect that story can have on our lives. Jim Loeher, one of the best performance psychologists in the world explains that we all live in the stories we tell ourselves.[8] According to Loeher and many other social scientists, when we see our present not working we can change the story of our future by telling ourselves a new story, one marked by hope.

The next step, and a crucial one, is to live out our future with hope, even when it goes against all odds (more about this in chap. 9). When we do this, we eventually experience changes in our real-time story. Paul may have had this in mind when he said, "May the God of hope fill you with all joy and peace as you trust in him, so that you may overflow with hope by the power of the Holy Spirit" (Romans 15:13).

I was impressed with how well a little guy with a purple crayon reflected my own story. The story reflected my view of life with such simple words that even a child could understand. Harold contributed to forming my value system. He has also empowered me to deal with the pain I was experiencing as a child. Did I resonate with Harold because of something already at work in me, or was I Harold's *tabula rasa*, his "blank slate"?[9] Probably a little of both. I do know that Harold made me realize that I could make my own story and live it. And I now covet that ability for others.

As I have been telling you about Harold, a childhood story of your own may have come to mind. If you do not remember a favorite childhood book, think about your favorite adult book or movie. These also reveal much about our value systems, which help us to understand ourselves and to better tell our stories.

My favorite adult book is *The Strange Case of Dr. Jekyll and Mr. Hyde*, which deals with the importance of keeping our inner life consistent with our outer life. Dr. Jekyll gave vent to his shadows by drinking a special recipe that caused him to temporarily change into Mr. Hyde, who had darker urges and even darker values. The two sides of the man warred for control over one body. Jekyll was horrified by what he had done and who he was becoming as Mr. Hyde. The dichotomy grew out of control, becoming worse with time. Jekyll spent less and less time as himself as Hyde began to take over. Dr. Jekyll did not believe he could get help. He confided in no one.

Eventually the only solution to the problem that Jekyll could accept was to kill himself, both Jekyll and Hyde. Much like Jekyll and Hyde, our inner voice and public voice can express two different stories. Integrity occurs when we freely speak a united truth, demonstrating that our inner life and public expression have become one and the same. The story of Jekyll and Hyde inspires me to hold personal honesty and integrity in highest regard.

A GUIDING LIGHT: YOUR FAVORITE QUOTE

Every follower of Jesus has a favorite Scripture or two. Many who do not follow Jesus have their favorites as well. Specific quotes float to the surface of our consciousness because they in some way define our values. They speak to the depths of what we believe is right and fair. They can also be inspirational and very often describe how we want to present ourselves in our world.

Favorite quotes are profound words that nudge us toward our best selves. Occasionally our favorite Scripture expresses a desire for some kind of comfort in response to our deepest pain. In most cases they are sage words that quickly come to mind when we are prompted to cite them. Therefore, they are key to discovering vocation because they quickly tell us what is important deep down inside, beyond our conscious minds. They perform the function of metaphor. A good metaphor gives you a snapshot of a larger concept in an image or a few words.

My favorite Scripture is from Isaiah 61:1-2 (see also Luke 4:18-19).

The spirit of the Sovereign LORD is on me,
    because the LORD has anointed me
    to proclaim good news to the poor,
He has sent me to bind up the brokenhearted,
    to proclaim freedom to the captives
    and release from darkness for the prisoners,
to proclaim the year of the LORD's favor

and the day of vengeance of our God,
to comfort all who mourn.

Isaiah 61 is important to me because it reminds me that based on my freedom as a prerequisite, I am anointed by God to carry a message. As I venture into the dark places where the poor, the captive, the blind and the oppressed reside, my voice becomes prophetic because it causes those in darkness to look up. Then God does God's part by bringing the year of the Lord's favor, a season of the gracious and abundant blessing of God.

Creating, adventuring, proclamation and liberating others stand in stark contrast to my former voiceless and small world. I am compelled to engage in spite of the negative prophecy over my life that tells me my voice is insignificant and will never matter. I still struggle with my physical voice, and sometimes it just barely works. It is a scar that will never go away. And it really should not disappear because my scars represent my best stories, which are stories of redemption. Creativity, adventure, proclamation and liberating others are my values that allow me to reach beyond that which limits me. Both Isaiah 61 and Harold embody these values and inspire me. Your favorite quote or book indicate your cherished values, which are pieces to the vocational puzzle. Although the role they play may not be clear to you right now, just humor me. You will soon understand.

REFLECTION AND PRACTICE

As you read about my favorite stories, your own favorite story may have come to mind.

1. What values did you learn from your story?

2. Do you have a favorite quote? What values do you notice when you read your quote?

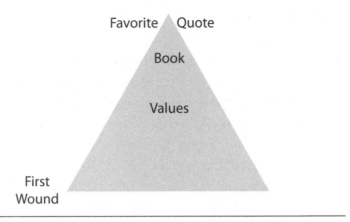

Figure 5.1. The vocational triangle

Add your favorite quote to the top peak of your vocational triangle (see fig. 5.1). Under your quote write the name of your favorite book. Note the values in your quote and book that resonate with you.

In chapter five you have discovered the second element in the vocational triangle, your values. In chapter six you will be working on the third element: your dreams for the sake of others. You will discover how they have the power to pull you forward into a significant life of vocation. You will see Joseph in a new light and meet my friend Bob, who, much to his delight, gave up financial success for the sake of some forgotten orphans.

-6-

Dreams That
Heal the World

Love yourself. Then forget it.
Then, love the world.

MARY OLIVER, *EVIDENCE*

I approached the front of the classroom and drew a huge dollar
sign, circled it and then drew a line through the circle on the
board. "What would you do if money was no object?" This was a
relatively ethereal question for seminary students who are trained
to think in terms of absolutes and of certainty about their doctrine
and practice. Since most grad students are overachievers, everybody
wanted to be able to answer my question. I could see it as they
leaned forward in their seats with anticipation. But nobody wanted
to be wrong. The pressure to respond was palpable. But what was
the right response? What did the professor want?

It wasn't that these students didn't have ideas. They had them for
sure. But who was going to risk missing the point? Who had
enough personal power to stake a claim? With eyes shifting from

left to the right, no one dared break the silence, and no one was making eye contact with me. The buzz of the fluorescent lights exacerbated the void. Their hesitance surprised me.

"All right then, take out a blank sheet of paper and clear your tables of computers and notebooks." I had read about something that might help to nudge students into right-brain creativity. "Write this at the top of your paper: '*My craziest idea for mission if money were no object.*' This should be an idea that you have fantasized about but never really brought out in the open. It will address these questions: What problem have you noticed in your world that you just can't shake, and how would you heal it? What unconventional approach would you take? How would Jesus show up through you in this situation?"

The pens moved sluggishly but eventually gave way to furious writing. Then, as instructed, the students handed their papers to the person on their left, who added their thoughts to their neighbor's *crazy* idea. The papers went around, gaining a contribution from each person that sat at the table. When the papers were returned to their owners, the classroom erupted with laughter and excited chatter.[1] The comments included everything from legal advice to offers of support, to irreverent jokes, to mock threats to call the police.

The students had understood the essence of the exercise and enjoyed the creative flow. I was thrilled. With their ideas quite literally out on the table, nearly everyone wanted to share their thoughts with the rest of the class. In the weeks that followed nearly 60 percent of these students successfully launched their *craziest "if money is no object" idea for mission* in their own communities.[2]

Money really wasn't an object for most of the participants because the bulk of our best dreams, in spite of what we tell ourselves, don't require much money. We tend to dream according to our uniqueness, and that even includes the size of our dreams. I have noticed that people with large dreams usually have the capacity to raise money for them. In the end, necessity *is indeed* the mother of invention. When hearts are impassioned, people can become amazingly resourceful.

DREAMING AND THE UPSIDE-DOWN KINGDOM

How would you respond to the questions asked of these seminary students? Does your imagination quickly stir? If it does, chances are that you are fluid with your dream factory. Each of us has the potential to dream, but for some the dream factory barely functions and for others it has shut down entirely.

The ability to dream is a quality that children possess without reserve. When Jesus said that we must become like little children to enter the kingdom of God, he meant that we adults have to recapture our innocence, our childlike faith and our ability to dream, and allow ourselves to be drawn forward into *wonder*.

We walk with God in a wide open space, an endless prairie, much like what the pioneers saw on their journey. It is God's prairie. The pioneers had to wrestle with nature, the land and themselves to bring shalom to earth in the form of their new home, the place of their dreams. Bringing shalom—and yes, you can equate that to vocation—down to earth right here and right now requires dreaming and wrestling. You will build on God's prairie what only you can build. However, in real time there are powerful and immediate realities that compete. Time and circumstance have their ways of snuffing out the dreams of the best childhood dreamers so that by the time we are adults we have learned not to dream, or we might say we have *unlearned* dreaming. This is actually not such bad news, because what we can unlearn we can also relearn. In order to do so we must develop a working relationship with play, risk and commitment. Our brain-writing exercise was an experiment in play. Risk and commitment come later in the doing phase.[3]

The hoped-for future cannot become a reality without the development of those dreams. Neither can a mission be fulfilled
without preparation. Typically, if adults are asked to dream about
some aspect of mission or vocation, they will bog down in the
process unless they are like my husband, Ken, who prolifically
imagines a hopeful future and always has his dreams ready to share.
For others the reality of everyday life grounds them to the reality
of here and now, and away from dream think and dream speak. But
if those same adults are asked what they would do for the sake of
others, the response will likely be more forthcoming and confident.
Dreams that exist for the sake of the other are easier to come up
with because they intersect with deep needs of our outer world.

The students from the seminary class were able to engage their
imagination quickly because they were asked to notice a need
around them rather than inside them. The needs of others are practical needs that often have a louder voice than our own inner needs.
They are less personal in many ways. What if in God's economy
your first pain was actually meant to be connected to your dream
to heal the world? What if all of your experiences are meant to
shape a vocation that God has designed especially for you? When
we dream for others, we are bringing our first pain in line with our
desire to heal the world, and in so doing we take the opportunity
to bring healing. We are becoming the change that we want to see.
This is how it has happened with me, my close friends who have
been with me in the development of vocation, and the many folks
who have been in my classes, workshops and coaching sessions. We
have become deeply engaged in our vocational story. And this will
also be the case for you as you journey along the vocational pathway.

Sharing our dreams with others is risky. If I want something for
myself and I dare to talk about it, how do I feel if it doesn't happen?

Foolish? Chagrined? Embarrassed? It is far more emotionally risky to request favors for myself than it is for others. Just ask any full-time missionary who has experience raising support. Asking for something for another person is much easier. Somehow it just feels less threatening, and in the end it is often more productive. Why is this true? The words of Jesus can bring some light to the matter. Jesus said, "Seek first his kingdom and his righteousness, and all these things will be given to you as well" (Matthew 6:33). He urges us to seek the kingdom of God before we think about our own needs. He adds, "Love the Lord your God with all your heart and with all your soul and with all your mind. This is the first and greatest commandment. And the second is like it: 'Love your neighbor as yourself'" (Matthew 22:37-39). Our dedication to the well-being of our neighbor is second only to our love for God, and in order to be the greatest we must become servant and slave (Matthew 20:26-28).

This upside-down kingdom that we have all heard about does make sense after all. Even though the natural impulse is to think of ourselves first, deep down most Christians intuit that putting others before ourselves is the right thing to do. Those who have the most fulfilling vocations have internalized this transcendent dynamic.

A WORD ABOUT DREAMING FOR YOURSELF

There is nothing wrong with having your own dreams. Our own dreams are the nexus of personal growth. Try becoming a success without first setting and then accomplishing personal goals. It is improbable that we could heal physical bodies without medical school, or build bridges without an engineering or architectural degree. I can think of many children who would not be alive if their parents didn't first dream about starting a family. Maybe your dream to travel the world will become the experience that will teach you intercultural skills. Those skills might erupt into a vocation in international relief. Following your dreams will likely lead you to dreams for others. We will be observing Joseph's life next. I doubt that Joseph would have had a plan ready for saving Egypt from famine had he not dreamed about rulership and thought about strategy. Esther would not have given herself so fully to the beauty call had she not dreamed of living a different life. Some of us are born with a drive toward the other. My husband, Ken, is like that. His earliest memories of getting in trouble in first grade were because he was defending an underdog on the playground. Others of us realize much later in life that we are designed to serve others. I am one of those. I was near midlife before I realized that dreams for the sake of others offered great rewards. Late bloomers can be just as powerful.

Dreaming is a process that of necessity evolves. In other words, dreaming leads to strategy. If you are not yet a fluent dreamer, don't become discouraged. Keep the important questions in mind. Love well. Pay attention to what is happening. And keep doing what is in front of you until you find success. The rhythm of the process will take you where you need to go next. Do not despise the rhythm, work with it and enjoy it. Accomplish your goals and then see where your dreams take you. Stay connected to those who see a future for you. If you give yourself to this process of vocational discernment now, you will likely get to your intended future much sooner than you might think.

AN EXPERIMENT IN DREAMING

Entertain this question for just a moment: For which people group do you feel compassion? For whom does your heart burst? What would you dream for the sake of those people? What would you do to bring healing to their broken world? Hang on to that thought while we take a look at a Bible story that illustrates the difference between dreaming for oneself and for the sake of others. This is the story of Joseph (Genesis 37; 39–50).

We first meet Joseph when, as a seventeen-year-old, he is exhibiting the cocky pride of a favorite son. Jacob, his father, had expressed his special love for Joseph by giving him an elaborate coat. Jacob showed a marked lack of parental wisdom by displaying an uneven love for his sons, and in doing so he deeply embittered Joseph's brothers. They did not appreciate Joseph at all. In fact, they hated him.

Everybody knew that Joseph was a dreamer. His dreams were literal sleeping-in-the-night type of dreams that mirrored his hopes for himself. Problematically, he had no emotional sensitivity as to how his dreams were being received by those around him, and this got him in a lot of trouble. Standing in the midst of his brothers wearing his *look at me I am the favorite son* coat, he proudly proclaimed that his family would one day bow down before him. This indiscretion nearly got him killed. Rather than murdering their brother, his siblings sold him off as a slave to passing Ishmaelites, who then sold him to Potiphar, an Egyptian. We can easily imagine the culture shock that young Joseph must have suffered. Being the favored one of his father's eleven sons, he was convinced that he was born for greatness. His dreams confirmed it. Life was good! How could this miscarriage of justice have happened? Under the watchful eye of his father, Joseph would have been groomed to rule. But faster than a cheetah pursuing its prey, providence in disguise chased him, caught him in its clutches and delivered him to an Egyptian taskmaster. Those dreams would have to be put on hold for now. But Joseph was not done with dreams.

In his subservient position Joseph did whatever he was given to do to the best of his ability. His talent for business was soon noticed. God was with Joseph and blessed him. Potiphar eventually trusted him with everything that he owned. Because Joseph was handsome, Potiphar's unfaithful wife wanted him. (I wonder how many of us can say that our incredible good looks played a part in determining the fate of our people.) When he turned her down, she falsely accused him of sexual misconduct. Off to jail he went. From an Egyptian prison Joseph contemplated his fate. His name meant "may Jehovah add or give increase." But rather than increasing, he was getting smaller. At least that is what his circumstances were prophesying to him. He was not acquiring cattle or servants, he was not free to marry and have children, and he was not gaining influence or power. He was not only a slave but an imprisoned slave. Could there be anyone more powerless? He had to wonder if God was mocking him. Twice Joseph had been in a position to step into his greatness, and twice defeat had dramatically and ironically snatched victory from him.

Imprisoned for what must have seemed like an eternity, Joseph again resigned himself to do whatever needed to be done to the very best of his ability. And once again, his business talent emerged, so much so that the warden trusted him with everything under his command, just as Potiphar had done. Joseph flourished in this role, and again God blessed him. Eventually another opportunity to distinguish himself appeared. And as before Joseph found himself working in dreams. He was able to interpret the cryptic dreams of Pharaoh's unfortunate baker and cupbearer. All that he predicted came true. His only request was that the king's servants not forget to put in a word for him.

Circumstances failed Joseph's expectations once again. As the story goes, the cupbearer forgot to speak up for him, which extended his stay in the jail for another two years.[4] But when Pharaoh needed help understanding his dreams, the cupbearer remembered, and Joseph was called to interpret. Pharaoh was pleased with Joseph's interpretation and also with the plan that Joseph strategically laid out before him. Joseph was now in charge of famine relief, which elevated him to the most powerful position in the land.[5] Did Joseph hesitate to accept this promotion? Was he afraid of another slapdown? Or rather, did he sense that this was the purpose for which he was born? He seemed to lurch forward, seemingly propelled toward risk, much like Esther.

Joseph became the savior of his people and also of all those who trusted in the grain stores of Egypt. What kind of ruler would Joseph have been had he not gone the route of sorrow and disappointment? Would he have been as strong and as willing to risk? Would he have been as determined and confident? Every twist and turn in his story, every hardship and disappointment that he faced became a powerful agent of change that challenged Joseph's character, molding him into the man that he needed to be. His vocation was served up to him on a sumptuous platter of humble pie that only twelve years in an Egyptian prison could deliver. By the time the king was having his dreams, Joseph was ready.

Did you happen to notice that by the end of his story Joseph was no longer proclaiming his own nighttime dreams? He became possessed by the waking dream of saving lives. He became a candidate for greatness when he allowed the locus of importance to pass from himself to others. Often we assume that our dreams are for our own self-fulfillment. But it is not in God's heart and mind to limit our dreams to just ourselves. In fact

> The world is already split open, and it is our destiny to heal it, each in our own way, each in our own time, with the gifts that are ours.
>
> TERRY TEMPEST WILLIAMS[6]

God has ideas, "For we are God's handiwork, created in Christ Jesus to do good works, which God prepared in advance for us to do" (Ephesians 2:10). There is an end in mind, and that end is the good works of serving others. How powerful would your life be if you began to allow the well-being of others to overtake your reason for existence? Next we will look in on Bob, a man who has been overtaken by his love for the most vulnerable.

BOB: JOYFUL ABDICATION OF WORLDLY SUCCESS

A chance meeting in a parking garage in downtown Portland brought Bob and me together. He was coming and I was going. Our mutual friend Billy introduced us, "Deborah, you have got to hear Bob's story." Billy knows how to incite my curiosity. After the formal niceties were out of the way, Bob briefly explained to me that he works with orphans in El Salvador. Then he said it—the statement that so intrigued me. "I love what I do so much that I would pay money to do this job." I knew I had to hear more from him, so later that month we Skyped, me from Portland, him from El Salvador.

Bob dreamed of running his own business. A math and physics degree didn't seem to be an appropriate segue to business ownership, so he dropped out of school, one semester shy of his degree, to pursue a career in sales. Bob's joyful can-do attitude was a natural foundation for his success in sales. He was good at it, very good. After working for ten or twelve different companies, he finally launched his own vending business. He served some of the largest corporations in the state, and his wealth grew exponentially as his company continued to expand. His dreams of running his own business and being financially successful had more than come true.

In the meantime, while visiting his wife's country of El Salvador he was unable to ignore the kids living on the streets. His heart began to break for them. Bob was once one of those kids who roamed the streets without parental supervision, lacking for love. He remembers the desperation, the pain and the loneliness. His deep joy became a quest to find secure homes for those unadoptable orphans with no place to call home. Bob searched countrywide to find the perfect live-in parents for the children. These homes have become places where the kids can grow to adulthood with love and acceptance. Schooling, spiritual mentoring and creature comforts are provided so that they can thrive and eventually make positive contributions to society.

Bob worked both his job and the orphanage concurrently for many years. Eventually his business became so demanding that he had to make a decision. Would he serve the orphans in El Salvador or would his business in Portland get all of his energy while someone else ran the orphanage in El Salvador? For Bob the decision was easy. His dream for his own life had transformed and he had lost his heart for business as usual. He found his deepest joy serving the kids, which he now does full time. This is a guy who said, "I didn't like sticky little kids that would get my white pants dirty." But then something changed. He gave up his business completely, and in that sense he does indeed pay money to do the work that he now does in El Salvador full time.

Bob started out with a dream for himself, which he accomplished. In his own words, his aha moment came when he realized that he had to follow the voice of the Lord telling him to "Go, sell your possessions and give to the poor. . . . Then come, follow me" (Matthew 19:21). With a laugh Bob advises, "Dump it. Go! You won't regret it!" I have never met anyone quite as joyful as Bob. When I asked him about his joy, he said, "When God smiles at you, you can't even move because the joy is so great. Combine all of your accomplishments and it doesn't compare to this joy. Success and money will never bring you happiness." Bob gave up his dreams of worldly success and responded to the call to dream for the sake of the other. The result? Great joy!

Joseph dreamed first for himself; then circumstances molded him into a dream facilitator for the sake of others. Bob dreamed first for his personal goals and then was drawn into a scheme orchestrated by God for the sake of vulnerable children in El Salvador. Two men worlds apart, centuries apart, and yet joined by a similar purpose and a call from God.

REFLECTION AND PRACTICE

1. What would you dream for the sake of the other? Who makes your heart break?

2. What would you do to bring healing to someone in this broken world?

3. If you were sitting at one of the tables with my students in the story at the beginning of this chapter, what would you write on your paper?

   Take a few moments and note your responses here.

4. Who do you know like Bob?

5. Name a few of their qualities that you admire the most.

6. What might you learn from him or her?

At the far right-hand corner of your triangle (see fig. 6.1), write down what you would do to heal our broken world.

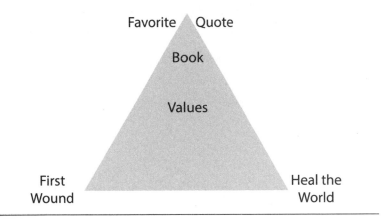

Figure 6.1. The vocational triangle

Creating Your Vocational Credo

There's a thread you follow. It goes among
things that change. But it doesn't change.
People wonder about what you are pursuing.
You have to explain about the thread.
But it is hard for others to see. . . .
You don't ever let go of the thread.

WILLIAM STAFFORD, "THE WAY IT IS"

W illiam Stafford, a United States Poet Laureate and Oregon State Poet Laureate, wrote "The Way It Is" a mere twenty-six days before he died. People tend to talk about what is most important to them just before they die. Stafford was a sage, a Janet Hagberg stage six sage, who seemed to be calling out continuity, commitment and the connectedness of all things. The thread you follow is continuous, and the one who holds onto it stays committed and connected. I like to think of Stafford's thread as a life that has been immersed in a relationship with God. The thread running through the hearts of both the Creator and the created. Might this be the significance that we all are looking for?

Up to this point in this book, you have read twenty-four examples of vocational credos, some are fully developed and some are not.[1] An idea may be percolating in your mind as to what this is all about, and maybe you are already working toward a rough draft of your own credo. Are you ready to make sense of all the thoughts that you have collected to create your credo? First allow me to give you my best explanation of the credo:

> A vocational credo is a description of personal passion directed toward a course of action that occurs for the sake of a specific outcome, that of doing good to and for others. It answers the questions, Why am I here? What do I uniquely bring? and, How can I help others? It leans heavily on empathy and hope. It is written in a format like this:
>
> *God created me (or I am on this earth) to* _____
> *so that*_____.

Although it is simple, and much like a mission statement or a vision statement in that every word is important, it is neither a vision statement nor is it a mission statement.

Once you have determined *why* you do what you do, your *what* and *how* will come easily. In different settings, *what* and *how* should change substantially as you grow and mature. If I were doing the same things today as I was doing when I was in my twenties or thirties, or even my forties, I would be underdeveloped and stuck. The nature and depth of the way that you live out your vocation grows as your spiritual depth and life experience increase. When I was in my thirties I facilitated others finding their voice through the physical expression of dance. I was a dance teacher.

Eventually what was once a legitimate outworking of my vocation no longer held my heart. As maturity set in I needed to flow with the seasons of my life, which required a deep change. A few college degrees later I am teaching and facilitating voice in a different way. We are designed to move on to greater depth internally as we mature, which means that sometimes what we do changes.

Greater depth does not mean a complicated or competitive lifestyle. Some folks focus their lives small and deep on purpose. They live an intentional life of spirituality and find fulfillment doing regular things like cutting hair, welding, running businesses, farming or teaching dance. A well-written credo will facilitate this too, as well as the growth and expansion of your vocation. Your credo will make room for your changing *what* and *how*. But at the core, your passion and your vocation will remain the same.

A few questions naturally tend to come up at this point, pushing back on the legitimacy of the credo concept. I will attempt to address them.

Isn't this struggle to find oneself a First World problem? It is sometimes suggested that my focus on vocation is an entitled person's concern. Some people assume that it is a struggle afforded only to those who hover near the top of Abraham Maslow's hierarchy of needs.[2] Maslow was a sociologist who charted the order and importance of human needs. It is pictured in figure 7.1, with the greatest need first and so on: physical needs, safety needs, love and belonging, esteem, and lastly, self-actualization.

The implication is that those who don't have their basic needs met, those who are underresourced or just barely making it financially, do not have the luxury or impulse to even think about vocation or higher meaning in life.

My critics assume that vocation is an act of self-actualization at the top of Maslow's hierarchy. It is certainly possible that vocation is a tension only for the affluent, who have the luxury of deciding what kind of work they prefer to do and when they prefer to do it. However this is rooted in the assumption that vocation is predominately income related rather than something that issues from

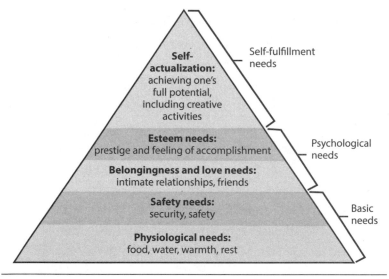

Figure 7.1. Maslow's Pyramid

our deep passions. Again, we might wonder, is deep passion a luxury? Actually, true vocation happens wherever people are present. In fact, it may be that those who achieve less in the world's view or earn less have the potential of doing the most meaningful work.[3] Great achievements do not necessarily translate into meaningful vocation. And mundane jobs do not necessarily translate into lack of meaning.

The locus of power of those who embrace power by achievement, according to Janet Hagberg, lies externally in what they have accomplished.[4] This is one of the lower stages of personal power, yet it is the most admired in our society. Gathering material possessions is the god of our culture. According to Hagberg, gold watches, fancy cars and large bank accounts are evidence of stage-three power. On the other hand, those who realize that power comes from within (stages four, five and six) cannot be controlled by exterior forces. Neither do they allow themselves to be defined by exterior forces.

If "vocation is about being raised from the dead, made alive to the reality that we do not merely exist, but we are 'called forth' to a divine purpose,"[5] then we must be able to exercise our vocation under almost any circumstance, otherwise God would have set up a situation in which very few could succeed, since most of the world struggles at the lower end of Maslow's hierarchy. I can't imagine why God would frustrate people in that way. It is not within God's character to do so.[6] Each of us as a child of God is created to succeed in our own way. Therefore vocation must be accessible to all.

The privileged can struggle with vocation as much as anyone. Complicated careers can demand so much of the soul that there may be nothing left for others. In fact, it might be argued that the more mundane the job or task, the simpler it may be to find transcendent meaning. An inner locus of power allows a person to develop an ability to act for the sake of the other, no matter what the job. In their book *Whistle While You Work* authors David Shapiro and Richard Leider begin six of their seven chapters with stories about taxi drivers who facilitate sage conversations while helping their passengers get where they need to go.[7]

We all know people like this. My dear friend Pam was a food lady at the local hospital.[8] She had a kind word of encouragement, affirmation or a secret prayer continually on her lips as she moved from room to room serving meals to the sick and dying. No doubt each person she served felt her gentle touch or experienced her grace. Now she works in a large cookie factory, another ordinary job. Pam expresses her creative side through collage art and blogging. She proudly proclaims her "ordinary personness," allowing all of us to see that a bright soul cannot be kept down by the mundane. Pam brings a spark of the divine to ordinary human situations, and in that moment comfort happens. Her example demonstrates that vocation is not just a privileged person's domain, but it can be found in any setting.

How do I live this out when I don't yet have a sense of wholeness in that area since it is rooted in my pain and weakness? This was my question in the beginning too. How do you *do* when you can just barely *be*? The answer lies in shifting focus and creating new habits of loving others no matter how we feel. When I was in India I was privileged to witness an act of love and generosity that I will never forget. Our bus stopped at a traffic light near a bridge. I noticed an older woman with crooked legs sitting on the sidewalk in the middle of the bridge. It was obvious that she could not move easily, someone must have dropped her off there to beg. She was extending her hand as people walked by, but she did not get much response.

Along came a man on a bicycle who was the thinnest person I have ever seen. His arms and legs looked like skin stretched over a skeleton, and he was eating something that looked like a sandwich. As the old woman extended her hand to him, he turned his head her direction but rode on by. Having second thoughts, he circled back, got off his bike and sat down with the old woman. Then he broke his sandwich in two and gave her a piece. The two sat there and enjoyed their common meal. He looked like he was starving himself, yet he had more than she did, and he shared it with her.

The light changed and our bus moved on but my heart didn't. For a long time I thought about what I had seen that day. In fact it still haunts me. One small event demonstrated to me that com-

forting those with the comfort I have received means that I have
to share the little bit more I have than the other person, whether
wisdom, education, time or just a sandwich. We are meant to walk
with a limp, all of us. We receive Jesus' strength when we are weak.
The apostle Paul tells us "power is made perfect in weakness"
(2 Corinthians 12:9). Jesus' love and strength shine through when I
conquer my fear and serve others regardless of my limp. Our
greatest leadership moments happen when we yield our pain to the
creative power of God.

*I have already written a personal mission and vision statement. Isn't
this good enough?* Someone often says, "I already know what my
vocation is. I wrote out my mission and vision statement at a conference." Good! I am glad that you did that! If you have taken the
time to write mission and vision statements, you have done some
deep work already. However vocation is not the same as mission or
vision, although it will eventually involve both.

Simon Sinek wrote a book called *Start with Why*.[9] He suggests
that companies need to know their *why* in order to be viable in the
marketplace, arguing that it is not good enough to merely have a
top-notch product. Companies that know *why* they are in the
business and *why* their product is important have the most impact
in the marketplace. As long as they stay on track with their *why*,
these companies are the most long-lived and the most effective in
the marketplace. From my experience with my own businesses, I
know he is onto something crucial here. Why wouldn't the same
be true for individuals? When we know our *why*, it becomes a
centering force for our lives, just as it is for businesses.

At a missions conference I was asked, on the fly, to talk about
sustainable mission. The question was, How might practitioners
create communities of faith that are sustainable for the long haul?
The audience was a group of pastors who were sent into the com-

munity to create new churches. They had all attended the mission-and-vision writing class months ago. They had returned to their contexts to live out their mission and vision statements, but when life and ministry got tough, their spirits flagged and they felt adrift. The most common questions were, How do we do sustainable mission? How do we not burn out?

I drew a huge question mark on the board along with the words *who, what, where, why, when* and *how.* They copied these words on a paper per instructions. Then they answered each of these questions for their own mission: Who do you want to attract? What will you do to make that happen? Where will you meet? Why are you doing this? When will you do it? How will it look? Although most questions were easily answered by either their vision or mission statement, nearly everyone failed to respond to the why question. They were confused by it. The most common answer was "for Jesus." And although true, everyone knew that was a lame answer. They knew there had to be more, but what was it?

Your *why* is absolutely core to your effectiveness. *You* now know what these pastors did not know at the time: vocation answers the why question. In small groups we worked through the steps of the previous chapters of this book. And they each discovered their *why* and wrote it out. The participants were stunned. They could see the potential for sustainability if they were doing what their hearts were compelling them to do, if they were doing their deep passion, if they were loving people for whom their hearts were bursting. Mission is sustainable when we know our *why.* This is not merely a corporate concept any more than mission or vision statements are solely corporate. Drawing on our deep well of passion sustains and renews our energy.

I don't see Jesus talking about vocation. What do you say about that? Jesus does not use the *vocation* word. But he does call us to a life of selflessness for the sake of others, which is the essence of effective vocation. He challenges us not to care about the little stuff.

> Consider how the wild flowers grow. They do not labor or spin. Yet I tell you, not even Solomon in all his splendor was dressed like one of these. If that is how God clothes the grass of the field, which is here today, and tomorrow is thrown into the fire, how much more will he clothe you—you of little faith! And do not set your heart on what you will eat or drink; do not worry about it. For the pagan world runs after all such things, and your Father knows that you need them. But seek his kingdom, and these things will be given to you as well. (Luke 12:27-31)

I find this Scripture very challenging because food and clothing are not inconsequential to me. I care a lot about my appearance. I consider dressing myself an art form. I don't want to trust God for my clothing. I want to choose my own. What if God and I have different tastes in fashion?

Not only that, but I live in Portland, Oregon, where excellent restaurants are found in abundance in almost every neighborhood. And we have adapted to our context. I confess that my husband and I are foodies. When we first started our church, my husband and I ate food bank donations for about four years because neither of us were getting paychecks. We both got chubby and very unhealthy. I care about what I eat. I mean, does God know that I am allergic? Does God know that I need to eat gluten free? Jesus is asking for a lot in this passage.

I know that I am being silly, but so often the desires of our flesh are just that—silly. However, there is a point here. Was Jesus only after temporal things, or was he addressing something deeper? Jesus never *had* to be hungry. After all, he turned water into wine and fed five thousand from a few fishes and loaves. Is Jesus hinting to his listeners that they could expect miraculous temporal provisions like he did?

Actually, rather than that, I think Jesus was trying to get at something much deeper than food or clothing. Jesus urged his listeners to make their treasure in heaven a top priority. A treasure in heaven is something that we would give our life for. The author of the book of Hebrews wrote of Jesus, who "for the joy set before him . . . endured the cross, scorning its shame, and sat down at the right hand of the throne of God" (Hebrews 12:2). Jesus had a single eye trained on us, which rendered him able to die an unjust death in order that we might be free, so that we could free others in turn. Jesus' deep gladness responded to the world's deep hunger. As it turns out, there are two kinds of hunger.

CREATING YOUR VOCATIONAL CREDO

Who do you care about the most? These are likely the people who will motivate you to heal the world. For me, they are voiceless people, which actually turn out to be mostly women and children, but also those who aren't in touch with their God-given purpose. And this usually includes more men than women. I resonate with these people because I once stood in their shoes. I know how it feels. These are the people that matter most to me. My heart bursts for them.

A good vocational credo responds to these questions: What would it look like if Jesus came into the midst of those I care about the most? How would Jesus' presence effect them? How would I act toward them if I were a representative of Jesus? The last question should help you find your action verb. Your action verb is directive. Here are a few examples of action verbs: *help, create, provide, facilitate, curate.* Check the list of vocations in appendix two for examples of these verbs.

Now it is your turn to write a vocational credo. Consider your first pain or wound, your favorite quote and book, and how you would heal the world. Your favorite quote and your favorite book highlight your values. Your first pain is the event or state of being that you eventually come to push back against. And your world-healing dream is connected to the people you care about the most, those your heart bursts for. All three are connected in the redemption of your pain and the expression of your values.

REFLECTION AND PRACTICE

Take a few moments to pray and ask God to help you. Then sit in silence. The Holy Spirit will guide your responses to these prompts.

1. How do you push back on your first pain?

2. How do your first pain and your impulse to heal the world interplay?

3. How do you see your values guiding your desire to heal the world?

4. What action verb will you use? "God put me on earth to [action verb] . . ."

5. Who will benefit from your vocation? Which people do you care about the most?

6. What would it look like for them if Jesus came into their midst?

If you struggle to find a connection, it might help to get someone else's eyes on it, someone you trust who knows you well.

Write your vocational credo on the next lines:

God put me on earth to_____

_____

so that_____

_____.

Try to get it down to no more than thirty words total. You will be memorizing your credo, so refine it until it says exactly what you want it to say in a way that rolls off your tongue.

Congratulations! You have finished the most challenging segment of this journey by creating your credo. You will massage this credo over the next few months and years so that it expresses your vocation exactly how you want it to. In chapter eight we will look at things that have the potential to derail your progress: Fear of failure and toxic skills.

- 8 -

Identifying Toxic Skills

Barriers to success are issues, either known or unknown to you, that will sabotage an earnest effort to live out your vocation. They are sometimes so hidden from us that we don't readily know what they are. They are rooted in risk aversion, lack of focus, confusion about vocation, failure to accept life as it comes, the desire to please, behavior disorders such as addictions and anger problems, untreated psychological issues, unrefined communication skills and wrong responses to stress and pain. Barriers to success may also be simply a lack of values or character. Most of these are fodder for the therapist couch and not in my scope of expertise. Rather, in this chapter and the next, I will present some ideas about toxic skills and fear of failure, which will address lack of focus and confusion about vocation and risk aversion, as well as an overdeveloped desire to please. These are the issues that most commonly sabotage an earnest desire toward vocation.

WHAT ARE TOXIC SKILLS?

Tunisia helps at her mother's home daycare. She loves children and would like to have a few of her own someday. She believes that she is called to love the little ones that have not been cherished, but she would love to do it in a different way. Tunisia has recently graduated from high school, and yet she has been working in the daycare for six years. She has something more in mind for the little ones than just caring for their bodies. Tunisia feels stuck, unfulfilled and confused as a daycare worker.

Nobody can calm a troubled child as easily as Tunisia. She has a gift that made her mother proud. Her mom did not understand why taking care of the children wasn't good enough for Tunisia. Mom was good at it too as a young girl. Why couldn't Tunisia follow in her footsteps? Childcare was good, honest work that faithfully paid the bills. But Tunisia was held captive by her "calling," or rather what she believed to be possible within the parameters of that calling. She secretly dreamed of creating an organization to help young girls find their value, enabling them to live out a different story than what they see around them. It became apparent to her that her gifts were more strategic in nature. Her ability to care for children, although good, was merely a starting point for bigger dreams. Her well-developed skill and the desire to please her mother stood in the way of what she really wanted to do. Until Tunisia found her voice and was able to tell her own truth well enough to articulate what she wanted, she was stuck in an unfulfilling job with toxic elements. But not any longer.

When I use the words *toxic skill*, people are immediately intrigued. Very few ask me what it means. Most know intuitively and connect to the idea emotionally with furrowed brow and a solemn nod. Toxic skills are skills that one does well, in fact, too well. It doesn't sound too bad does it? The problem is that, in the doing, they bring us no life or energy. They have the potential to actually kill us, which is why they are sometimes referred to as "killer skills." If it's toxic to us, it's a toxic skill. They suck life from our soul and

sometimes our body. For instance, when I pay my bills I get a satisfaction from the completion of the task. I am happy when it is
done. I am intuitive with money and accounting skills, but I hate
doing the job. I do it well, even though it is a hellish experience. I
am convinced that it drains the blood from my face, and afterwards
I am pale, hollow-eyed and sweating profusely.

The only other alternative to me doing the bills is my husband.
He handled our finances a few times, which was a disaster. The
financial ship listed dangerously to starboard and we almost sank.
He does other tasks so much better. In the end he suggested that I
do the bills, because of my natural gift for accounting. I am happy
to contribute to my family in that way. It is a means to an end: financial security. Although I must pay the family bills, it would not
be wise to choose accounting as my vocation. I had an accounting
practice for eighteen years and it nearly did me in. What kept me
alive was my friendships with my clients. Accounting served its
purpose in my life for a season when I needed good pay and flexibility. When that season was over I could not get out of the profession quickly enough.

In contrast, when I get my hands into the soil to plant flowers,
or when I am harvesting my herbs, I am in heaven. I feel connected
to the earth and to the Creator. I love every bit of the process, from
shopping for seedlings to cooking with what I have harvested. The
smells, the touch, the joy, all cause me to look forward to spring
when I can fill my many pots with plants and seedlings. Gardening
brings me pleasant satisfaction. I do admit to a little bit of a black
thumb every now and then, but it really doesn't matter. For me,
gardening is the opposite of a toxic skill. I don't have to be good at
it; I just have to enjoy it. Many would say that I should do what I
do best and leave the rest to someone else. I would argue that I
should do what I enjoy, regardless of how well I do it, and leave the

rest undone. Vocationally, it could be a good choice to open a plant shop or an herb shop. I would use my accounting skill in a small way and engage my entrepreneurial urge and my love of growing food and flowers.

Sometimes it takes a while to discover what toxic skills are. If you feel lifeless or depressed after a specific activity, you might have discovered a toxic skill. They are abilities that have the capacity to keep you locked into your own smallness. When limited to a toxic skill, you are not free to discover more pleasurable pastimes or greater gifts. I am not suggesting that we never do those things that are distasteful to us. Each of us has something like this in our lives. Each skill that you identify as toxic is actually meant to be a tool in your tool belt to accomplish something greater. Do not discard these tools.

I am suggesting that we become aware of what brings and does not bring life to us emotionally so that when we step into the job market we do not commit forty hours a week or more to something that is not emotionally sustainable. Short term, however, we may need to do any number of jobs that we do not enjoy. Paying the bills, keeping a roof overhead and purchasing food are necessary. Keeping alive the dream of a better day and sustaining the space in your heart for what gives you joy is the key to functioning in less inviting areas of endeavor.

Toxic skills are abilities that bring little or no life to us, which have the power to keep us locked in our own smallness if we do not think critically about them.

Three clues alert us that a toxic skill is rearing its dreadful head. First, shame is a sign that we may be tempted to or are doing something that is toxic. When folks understand that we know how to do something well, they often expect us to do it whether it is good for us or not. For example, I am typically expected to pick up the accounting chores in most organizations I am closely involved with. I do not do this, but I often feel shamed for not participating in the expected way. Shame often causes us to say *yes* when we should be saying *no*. I responded with a lot of yeses before I learned how to say no.

Avoidance is the second sure-fire clue that we may have a toxic skill. It might be a clue when we put off a task until the very last minute, or if the task drifts to the bottom of the to-do list day by day and week by week.

Refusing to tell others about a skill is another sign of toxicity. I went to school for fashion design. I know how to do everything from hemming a pair of pants to designing a dress and drafting its pattern. For years I did not tell anyone this, because if I did, I would be asked to replace broken zippers and hem jeans. If we keep a skill a secret so that nobody asks us for help in that area, it's probably a toxic skill.

THE GIFTS OF TOXIC SKILLS

Toxic skills are actually gifts that God has given us. However, they have been allowed to overstep their intended bounds. It will help us to consider that they are actually a means to an end. We are meant to use them as tools. For example, if you were building a bench, you would not consider the saw to be more important than the finished project, would you? Likely not. The finished bench would be the thing of beauty, not the saw. The saw is merely a tool to accomplish the task of making the bench.

I am an entrepreneurial artist, as well as an extrovert who has never met a stranger; they are merely friends that I don't yet know. I have started seven businesses in my adult life. I need the skills of mathematical proficiency, investing and accounting in order to allow new churches, dance schools and other organizations to thrive.

They are tools for my broader, more strategic vocation of helping people find their voice. Accounting skills are like the bench-building saw, they are tools meant to fade into the background.

Tunisia eventually used her knowledge, experience and empathy, which was her saw, for the little girls in her mother's daycare. These tools helped her to develop programs that build the self-esteem of preteen girls. Her years in the daycare were not wasted.

Your toxic skill is someone else's joy, and your joy is someone else's greatest nightmare. I had a business partner who really hated talking in front of a crowd. Conversely, I come alive when I am in front of a crowd. She loved administration, which makes me break out in hives. She was excellent, creative and fast. I am unable to make anything on the back end of a website work right. But my partner could. I have another friend who is actualized, as in a spiritual experience, when she balances the books. Financial statements are her Van Goghs. She draws great satisfaction from making it all work. There is someone who really loves to do that which is toxic to you. Make it your opportunity to find that person. You will be happier, and so will he or she!

REFLECTION AND PRACTICE

It is important for the process of vocational discovery that you take the time to find out what your toxic skills might be. Think back to work situations, including paid work, volunteer work and work in your home. Note a few situations that feel toxic to you. Sometimes those around you can help you tease out what you do well but at the same time dislike doing, so ask for help if you need it. Think as specifically as you are able and then respond to these questions:

- What do I do well that I don't talk about?

- What specific tasks cause me to procrastinate?

- What is it about this task that I avoid?

- Under what circumstances do I find myself saying yes on the outside and screaming no on the inside? What is it about this task that causes this reaction?

As you have been reading these words, something has likely come to mind.

1. What toxic skill is a tool that has overstepped its bounds in your life?

   Note that here:

2. How has it stood in the way of you doing what you really want to do?

   On a clean piece of paper create a job timeline, including everything that you have done for work, both paid and volunteer. Under each job list the skills that you used. Write in blue those that you enjoyed and in red those that you did not enjoy. Circle those that might be toxic skills.

3. What did you learn about your toxic skills from this exercise?

4. Note the crossover of toxic skills you listed earlier with the ones you listed here.

5. Summarize what you have learned about yourself here.

Chapter eight has brought your toxic skills to light. This should be refreshing information and a tool to help you form your future. It should be a relief to know that you can now put these skills in their place. In chapter nine we will discuss another barrier to success that can be a positive player in your future: fear of failure.

9

Addressing the Fear of Failure

At the core of many barriers to success is a relationship to failure that drives emotional or moral collapse in some way. On the wild frontier, fear of failure is both life-preserving and life-damning. However, just as with toxic skills, failure has a golden side. I will attempt to tease out its benefits.

THE FAILURE CLUB

Have you ever heard of a failure club? Perhaps not. As I began to ponder failure I remembered that

> Only those who dare to fail greatly can ever achieve greatly.
> ROBERT F. KENNEDY[1]

some expert once said that success helps us to do the same thing over and over again while adding nothing new. For a creative person such as myself, lack of surprises along with endless repetition are nails in my coffin. I apparently need the challenge that failure presents, because I surely experience a lot of it. According to social scientists, failure brings new understandings. However, contemplation is needed to appreciate all that it has to offer.

Failure has helped me to answer these questions: Why do I sail over the edge of respectability and embarrass myself? What causes me to give up? Why do I lie? What stimulates my greed? There are other less-character-intensive failures too, such as, Why didn't anyone show up for the work party? Why was that event such a flop? Why didn't that product sell?

As I contemplated what failure has to offer, I began to wonder why we don't listen to the voice of failure and court its wisdom as a cherished friend. It's a little counterintuitive, I admit, and definitely risky, but so intriguing! So I decided to start a failure club. Failure is so widespread, I thought, that many people might even want a charter membership. At the very least they would show up at meetings to commiserate. We could talk about everything from community project failures to church failures to moral failures. Here was my idea: Create an atmosphere where the attendees could bring their biggest disasters to the table. Or maybe they would bring a situation where they got stuck. Or they might want to discuss those glitches that keep them from forward movement on their projects. Each person would share what they learned from their own personal debacle. The group then would act as accountability partners, brainstormers and supporters to help each other accomplish success in their next attempt. We would all learn from the failures of others as well as our own. What a rich learning experience this could be. I was sure that my failure club was a brilliant idea and bound for success. The problem was that no one showed up to the meetings. Admittedly, it was a very hard sell. It seems that the word *failure* kind of puts a damper on any entrepreneurial or character-growth enthusiasm.

My failure club was an epic failure.[2] Maybe some rebranding would help: *"Failure Club: The Place Where Everyone Knows Your Name."* Or *"The Place Where People Celebrate Hard Lessons Learned."*

Or *"Divided We Stand, United We Fall."* No one loves to fail, especially me, and I am certainly not advocating failing on purpose. But sometimes we are so afraid of failure that we never try. We just don't want to think about it in our success-oriented culture. So when people fail, it swiftly gets swept under the carpet as an undiscussable. No one wants to talk about their negative experience. But what if we did discuss it? Unless we develop a constructive relationship with failure, we run the risk of being locked in a prison of our own making, a prison of unfulfilled dreams and fear, a prison where we never glean wisdom from our failures.

RISK, FAILURE, SUCCESS

Living into your vocation demands trial and error, and thus risk. Risk exists in a continuum between opposites: failure and success. Success is simply not available without the possibility of failure. The degree to which we risk failure is the degree to which we have the possibility of succeeding. A healthy relationship to failure is not merely a flight of fancy but a necessity. Check out the following people who between them had 15,126 failures.

Thomas Alva Edison, the inventor of the light bulb, was a classic *failure-to-success* kind of guy. He was famously known for saying, "I have not failed. I've just found ten thousnd ways that won't work. Many of life's failures are people who did not realize how close they were to success when they gave up." Edison failed epically! Veiled not too thinly in this quote is Edison's bow to the need for failure as part of the success plan. The light bulb was one of the greatest inventions of his century. But what if he had quit at ten thousand tries? It's a round number; it would have made sense.

Another *failure-to-success* guy is James Dyson, who invented the Dyson vacuum cleaner.[3] He made 5,127 prototypes before he was satisfied. That means that 5,126 were, well, not quite right. They were failures on some level. His vacuum cleaner now sits in the design hall of fame. It is not only a superbly functioning vacuum but an artistic one as well. And he is on to inventing all other kinds of neat household tools. Both of these men risked big, failed big, 15,126 fails between them. And then they won in epic fashion. But there was no success without first failing.

MORAL FAILURE

Moral failure is discussed in the book of Proverbs, "though the righteous fall seven times, they rise again, but the wicked stumble when calamity strikes" (Proverbs 24:16). This does not mean that a person only gets seven tries. Biblically, analysts say that seven is the number of completeness. This means that however many times we need to fall before succeeding, we have those falls. Let me say that again: tries times infinity is what we get. Will we need that many? Probably not, but if we do, the provision is there. The key is getting back up. The only way a person can fall again and again is if he or she gets back up again and again. The wicked are brought down by calamity. When those who fall do not attempt to get back up, they have no chance to succeed. The conclusion of the proverb: Rather than a clean track record of always doing right, it is human to fall and get back up. This is what makes a person just before God. Wow! Could this be God's view of failure? I certainly hope so. Proverbs gives us an insightful view of what determines success. A multitude of failures are acceptable as long as I conclude with just one success. It was the same for Edison, Dyson and the sinner—many tries, just one success needed!

Author William Saroyan resonates with the writer of Proverbs. He says, "Good people are good because they've come to wisdom through failure. We get very little wisdom from success, you know."[4] Rather than an endorsement for failure, Saroyan is urging his listeners to find the richness in failure. Failures can become friends that push us toward our goals rather than defeat us. If, when we fail, we decide, "I will never try that again," we will be locked in at that juncture. The eventual result will be crippling fear that becomes a barrier to success. In failure we find both fear and the potential for growth. Each one of us gets to choose for ourselves which is more important.

The vocational pathway often provides no road signs, therefore experimentation is necessary. A paralyzing fear of failure does not play well in this arena. The process of trial and error supports the development of new understandings. The learner discerns which practices are useful and which are not. The brain-writing exercise in chapter six was meant to push those practitioners beyond their known safe territory to a place where any flight of imagination found support and therefore became *possible.* The comments from their fellow students allowed them to adjust their ideas so they might become *viable.* What would your vocation look like if you were empowered in this way? What if fear of failure was taken off the table? What if you were allowed as many failures as you needed to accomplish your goal? What would you do?

REFLECTION AND PRACTICE

1. What was your family culture related to failure?

2. Name your emotions around your own failures.

3. Write down any failures that you have experienced that might be standing in the way of your success today.

10

Pursuing Change and Chaos

Chris was a Midwest girl who had been drawn to Washington, DC, as much for an escape from her childhood home as for the ample cultural opportunities that it offered. A tall beauty of only twenty years, she was fast-tracking toward a career in high-fashion modeling after moving to the big city. Although this career choice has been successful, fulfilling and exciting for many, it was not a good fit for Chris. Chris often spent her weekends and evenings at the theater or the symphony. Soon after moving to Washington, she attended the National Symphony of Dvorak's *New World Symphony*. As the music moved her deeply, she had an aha moment. While contemplating the meaning of her life, Chris realized that she could never fully embrace the lifestyle of a model. It was too frivolous for her. She felt compelled to dedicate her life to pursuits that would change the lives of others in substantial ways. After that night Chris broke up with the modeling agency and allowed her deeper interests to guide her toward intellectual pursuits and meaning.

Some years later a mentor asked her the vocation questions:

What makes you weep? What makes you pound the table? What keeps you awake at night? As she contemplated her responses to these questions, she was moved to shift gears once again. "Poor leadership keeps me awake at night, and it makes me very angry," she replied without skipping a beat. A woman of action, Chris went back to school to study communications and leadership, earning a bachelor's, a master's and then a doctoral degree. Since then Chris has founded a school, written and taught leadership curriculum on nearly every continent in the world, and is now the president and founder of a nonprofit after-school program for kids from low-income neighborhoods, which teaches character skills through the practice of art.[1]

Chris has made deep change a habit. Deep change requires a willingness to throw life into chaos for the sake of the next stage of development for either oneself or someone else. Robert Quinn calls it "walking naked into the land of uncertainty."[2] This presents a viscerally vivid picture, doesn't it? Quinn asserts that incremental change is not effective when it comes to human beings and human systems. Deep change requires an all-or-nothing commitment. Folks need a life-jolting shift to become something other than what they currently are. They do not change their circumstances unless it becomes untenable to remain stagnant. It became obvious to Chris that her relationship with the modeling agency was toxic to her soul. She severed her relationship with her known future, setting herself adrift while she waited for the unknown to emerge.

THE CHAOS MODEL: A JOURNEY OF FAITH

Knowing where you want to go and having a practical, known pathway there are two different things. The essence of faith is letting go of the little value still resident in the known and having nothing of substance to grab onto. Faith has eyes that can only see in the dark. If you can see it, your emotional response might be that of expectation or hope, but it is not faith. Faith is an assurance of things not seen (Hebrews 11:1). So how does one move practically from faith to working out vocational goals? What are the steps?

A few years ago my husband and I were facing a change of circumstances that thrust us from our beloved family home, most of our friends and family, and our church. We landed in a city that was new to us. We didn't know many people, how to get around, or where to go for medical care or even where to buy groceries. Not only that, but we went from earning predictable paychecks to living by faith.

We felt prompted to start a church counterintuitive to tradition, that is to say unique.[4] We found no supporters among the churches of our city, and I don't blame them. We were so outside of the box that we needed to prove ourselves, and that would take time. So both our newly started church and our family would trust God for provision. Living by faith was the last thing in the world we ever wanted to do. I am a bottom-line person, and I need the money to make sense. If the money path isn't clear, I am insecure and perfectly capable of sharing my angst with everyone—not a pretty sight!

> As we embark on a new creative venture, it helps to remember that we are working with a God who loves us more than anything in the world.
>
> ELLEN MORRIS PREWITT[3]

A friend from afar rescued us from our fearful wonderings with some sage words and a picture, which turned out to be one of the best pieces of advice we have ever received. He drew a chaos model (more on this in a moment) on a napkin and said, "Remember this." The image that he sketched for us has helped us to hang on to God in the midst of deep change when life seemed bleak in every way.

The surface story, the official truth, was that we were being sent out to church plant. But there was a nasty underbelly. The real story, the ground truth, was that we were fired from our jobs. We were deemed misfits for the pastoral team because our vision was different from that of the senior pastors. Although at first it was very painful for us and unexpected, very soon we came to realize that *God* was moving us toward our vocation, which was far more interesting and dynamic than being asked to leave. We realized that although we were not in control of our future, God was. In the meantime, we clung to a little diagram that our friend drew on a napkin. It had instantly made so much sense that we couldn't forget it. Since that time we have shared this diagram with hundreds of people, and it has helped them too.

The chaos model is another way to understand how to embody what God has already said to us and about us in the Bible. Much like the Hebrews escaping Egypt, God did not bring us out of our captivity to tease us or to send us back, even though at times it felt that way. God was coaxing us forward. God's thoughts toward us were good and were intended to bring us a great future where our hopes and dreams wouldn't fizzle or be snuffed out (Jeremiah 29:11).

To help you understand the confusing circumstances that will likely present themselves to you I suggest you develop your own personal mentor board. As the Bible points out, there is wisdom in a multitude of counselors. A natural human tendency is to isolate ourselves when faced with challenging adaptions to life, whether they are intentional or not. A well-designed proactive plan may substantially amend our outcomes. This is the genius of a mentor board. They are a few, maybe five, people who will walk gently yet strongly with us. They become our cheerleaders. They trust our own process for change, yet they have an instinct for what will be problematic as well as what will work. They are not afraid to speak up. But they do so in a way that we can hear their concerns and encouragements. My mentor board includes a broad age range. My teenage granddaughter keeps me rooted in reality on a visceral level, and my septuagenarian friend speaks to the depths of my heart. The key thought is this: *Who can help me with wisdom that will help me move forward in the best way possible no matter what the circumstances?*

So here is the piece of brilliance that I have been telling you about.

THE CHAOS MODEL

We will work through the stages of change starting at the bottom of the diagram and moving upward (see fig. 10.1).[5]

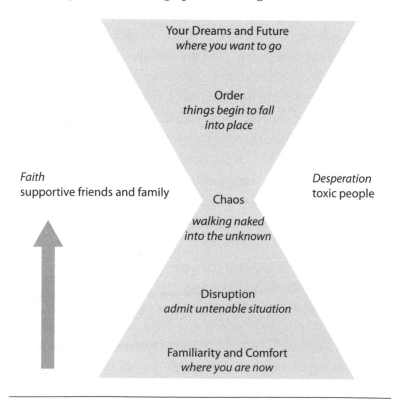

Figure 10.1. The chaos model

1. The beginning is a place of relative *familiarity and comfort*. Eventually, you have come to realize that it is not where you want to be. Through circumstances both internal and external, you realize that you want more for your life than you are able to get where you are, or circumstances overtake your life as they did with Ken and me. You feel the urgency for change. You *admit* to yourself that change is imminent and unavoidable.

2. You head toward the state of *disruption* by quitting your job, moving to another city or whatever you need to do for change. Intentionally or otherwise, you are compelled to move forward. You realize that accomplishing your dream could be a reality. Consequently, this large-scale plunge sets in motion a series of many smaller ripples that disrupt your life and move it toward a state of *chaos*. Nothing remains as it was. At this point it is helpful to find people who believe in you and will support your goals. I have a mentor board of supportive advisers whose wisdom I seek before I embark on any deep change. Sometimes deep change is thrust on us, and we find ourselves in chaos. My mentor board helps me with the unexpected and intentional disruptions in my life.

3. You walk *naked into uncertainty*, with *chaos* looming in the distance. Emotionally this stage is a minefield. Circumstances are getting tighter and tighter by the day, but you are resolutely moving forward. You might feel like either failure or death is imminent. Your *supportive friends and family* help you to stay focused by reminding you of your *why* by praying for you and by empathetically listening to you. You will draw strength from them as you learn what works and what doesn't. You scramble to make your day-to-day existence viable. Scrambling is an important skill for those of us who live a life of deep change. Scrambling consists of doing whatever it takes to make life work. In order to scramble,

you have to set your ego aside, because it might require living on food stamps, asking for help or working at McDonald's.

4. At the bottleneck, you are living in total *chaos*. *Desperation* is on one side and *faith* is on the other. In this phase people often feel a little schizophrenic. They bounce back and forth between "did I just make the biggest mistake of my life?" and "I see a future on the horizon for me, and I am excited about it." When the squeeze is the tightest, surround yourself with those who encourage you. Let go of toxic relationships. Toxic relationships are made of those people who tell you that dreams are too risky and that you will fail. These people need too much from you. They are the opposite of your personal mentor board. Sometimes it is merely a decision to get rid of these folks in your life. However, this may be a family member who you do not have the luxury of editing from your life. Therapists are good resources to help you learn how to manage the negative words and energy they send your way.

5. As you pass through the bottleneck, you begin to find new rhythms. This happens because human beings are creatures of habit. We want life to be *ordered*. The stress will ease up as you see yourself getting life back into a manageable order and advancing toward your goals. *Order begins to return.*

6. Your big picture has changed now. As the details of your life normalize, you will find that you have arrived at your destination, the *future* that you *dreamed* of, and hopefully you will be closer to living out your vocation. Your estimated time of arrival at your new Shangri-La will most likely be measured in months and years, not hours and days. Patience proves to be a virtue.

People who have become comfortable with risk and failure will dive into the chaos model numerous times in their lives. When Chris made her decision to live with meaning, it meant that she was choosing the chaos model as a lifelong companion. And that has proven to be true for her. In the years that I have known Chris, she has journeyed the route of chaos on a semi-regular basis. It hardly seems painful to her anymore, at least from the outside. Many folks, however, have neither the fortitude it takes to fight through nor the support they need to come out the other side. When the challenge gets too great, they circle back down to *familiarity and comfort* at the bottom of the diagram, and convince themselves that it wasn't so bad there after all. Many times throughout life they may circle between *comfort* and *chaos* without success, sensing that there is a breakthrough just ahead but too confused or frozen with fear to complete the process. If this is you, my desire is that you have garnered hope from what you have read. If the notion of the wild frontier excites you, start your journey by engaging a mentor board. You will not regret it!

When I know I am heading into a chaotic time of change in my life, I make sure that all the pieces that I can control are in place. Remember the *wild frontier*: it is as close as your heartbeat and as far as your fears. My fears stretch out like the legs on a daddy longlegs spider. I am not short on fear. Knowing that God is helping me find a pathway forward in my life eases my angst and allows me to stay in the process, though it is painful. I am blessed to have the support of friends and family who will cheer me on when the going gets rough. I minimize my exposure to toxic people, those who need too much from me or who routinely predict my disaster. These preparations have proven to be invaluable.

Finding and developing your vocation requires constantly returning to that place of risk, growth and faith. Each time you journey the pathway, it becomes more familiar and eventually will become your old friend. I can't say that I have ever been disappointed as I have given myself to the process of the chaos model. I don't always get what I expect, though. In fact, sometimes the outcome is a complete surprise. But I love to be surprised. Surprises stand in stark contrast to the sameness of everyday living and provide impetus for growth, which helps me toward a greater expression of vocation and usefulness to others.

Certainly there are many unforeseen circumstances that threaten to take a person out of the game. Many are legitimate. If you should fall out of the game, give yourself a break to rest and recuperate, and then jump back in as soon as you can. The chaos model is not a fail-safe system that promises delivery into the idealized future, but it may come close. By developing an awareness of how change works through pain and chaos, you can learn how to focus on that which is significant and let the rest go.

REFLECTION AND PRACTICE

1. Name a time when you experienced the chaos of change. Did you make it through to the new life that you had been hoping for? If so, how? If not, describe what happened and what you would do differently.

2. Identify your toxic relationships. What will you do to manage those relationships?

3. Write down the names of those you would like to be on your mentor board, and write their job description. Make a date to talk with each of them.

11

Discovering Your
Vocational Preferences

By now you know that vocation itself does not come from a job, schooling or a common-sense choice, but by exploring the history of your life to discover what your passions and painful events have to reveal to you. And you have done a substantial amount of work by writing your vocational credo. The Vocational Preferences Survey is a way to dial in to how that vocation might be lived out in a way that is most fulfilling for you. In the grand scheme of *why, how* and *what,* this will be your *how. How* do you best live out your vocation? It is akin to a vision statement.

There are ten vocational preferences in this survey. You may think of others that apply to you, but I am using these ten because they are the most common preferences I have discovered in my research. I designed this survey in a way that will allow you to uncover your top two or three motivators, your best *how.* It is possible to have a deep joy for a specific work and yet not know how to best practice it. Your *how* allows you to find the proverbial sweet spot in your meaningful work. Another benefit of working within your vocational preferences is that your efforts will be sustainable.

You will be working in the manner that is most natural and enjoyable for you.

Go to appendix three of this book and follow the instructions for the survey. When you have finished, return to this page and write your top two or three preferences here:

In the following paragraphs you will find a description of each category with examples of how they might look in real life. I have noted the core motivation, which will help you understand why you might express vocation in that certain way. I list possible pathways as a few of the avenues that I have seen each vocational preference expressed. This is not an all-inclusive list, there are many more. Every vocational preference has inherent weak areas, so I list a few possible hindrances to success. These are, again, only a few ways that people might fall out of sync with their vocational journey.

Read through the preferences, underlining those that you have listed as your top two or three categories. If you have a tie, choose the preferences that most excite you. You will use these in the next exercise.

Caregiver. *A caregiver finds deep satisfaction in helping the young or old, the socially or financially challenged, or the disabled with their basic needs.*

- *Core motivation.* Seeks to make the world a better place by improving life for just one person.

- *Possible pathways.* Daycare provider, care to the elderly or disabled, nurse, doctor, driver, personal services, minister, spiritual director, counselor.

- *Example.* Markus has always found deep satisfaction no matter the kind of work he was doing. In every situation he has found people to love and care for. As a minister he tends to his small flock of twenty-five congregants. He knows each person by name, and he knows their stories. When he was working as a mail carrier, he "brought sunshine and cheerful words" to the people on his route. Markus's current second job is caring for elderly folks. He says, "I find deep satisfaction in making one day better for each person in my care." Markus's passion is to invest himself in others through one-on-one interaction.

- *Potential hindrances to success.* Burnout, overcommitment, not caring for one's own needs.

Connector. *A connector loves to create venues where people can find common ground, whether to learn, have a meal, share a common cause or to just enjoy each other's company.*

- *Core motivation.* Seeks to make the world a better place by getting people together to interact with each other.

- *Possible pathways.* Party organizer, events coordinator, hostess, book club host, teacher, community facilitator.

- *Example.* Sarita might be called a modern-day matchmaker. In the last year she has turned her talent for creating events into a moneymaking proposition by hosting dinner parties for single women and men so they can get to know each other in a genteel, nonthreatening atmosphere. For single parents who rarely make it to their church on Sunday, Sarita hosts a religious service twice a month during lunch hour at her nine-to-five job. She is passionate about connecting people with each other and connecting people with God.

- *Potential hindrances to success.* Getting caught up in systems and structures; forgetting that it is supposed to be fun for everyone, including oneself; losing a sense of play.

Creator. A creator loves the metaphoric and symbolic, expresses deeper meaning through atmosphere, which is created, often without words, through stimulation of the senses.

- *Core motivation.* Seeks to make the world a better place by expressing beauty, emotion or disruption through art.

- *Possible pathways.* Artist, craftsperson, designer, musician, cook, woodworker, interior designer, filmmaker, writer, comedian, hostess, photographer, social program designer, curriculum designer.

- *Example.* As a part-time art teacher, Joni notices beauty in the simple things of life. She also finds humor in the mundane. Joni makes short films—music only, no dialogue—that make people smile. She volunteers at the local high school helping students to write scripts for their own film projects. Joni says she feels her best when she is "collaborating with my friends to create public art installations." Her passion is empowering others to create art that evokes emotion.

- *Potential hindrances to success.* Getting so caught up in the creative process that one becomes self-consumed; living as a starving artist and not taking care of everyday life; forgetting that the end purpose of vocation is altruistic.

Communicator. A communicator carries a message and will use any avenue to make sure the person or people on the other end receive it.

- *Core motivation.* Seeks to make the world a better place by learning, teaching, showing or demonstrating in order to bring new thoughts or experiences to others.

- *Possible pathways.* Educator, writer, life coach, artist, craftsperson, designer, musician, songwriter, comedian.

- *Example.* Tressa is a spoken-word artist. She carefully crafts messages meant to provoke deeper thoughts and feelings about issues that matter to her. Tressa is writing two books, one for her poetry and another to help others develop their poetic voice and performance style. Tressa is both a guest instructor and performer at a local high school, where she helps students find their voice. Tressa's passion is to help others learn new ways to communicate meaning.

- *Potential hindrances to success.* Falling into the role of teacher and forgetting to be a learner, not listening.

Problem solver. *A problem solver thinks and experiments their way through problems.*

- *Core motivation.* Seeks to make the world a better place by pioneering solutions and creating pathways to success; helps others understand complicated problems.

- *Possible pathways.* Engineer, scientist, researcher, doctor, physicist, community sage, handy-person, specialist in remodeling houses, business owner, scholar, idea person.

- *Example.* Malcolm is a software engineer who writes for a local design firm. His eyes light up when he is given an "unsolvable" project. Malcolm is also an adventurer, as many problem solvers are. In his spare time he likes to explore the backroads of America. He says he loves to "go to the edge." Malcolm's passion is finding pathways to do things that were once impossible.

- *Potential hindrances to success.* Leaving people behind in the pursuit of the adrenaline rush, forgetting that there is always a person at the end of the problem at hand.

Helper. *A helper assists others in doing what they want to do, often through physical labor or by the giving of resources.*

- *Core motivation.* Seeks to make the world a better place by doing for others what they cannot do for themselves.

- *Possible pathways.* Philanthropist, fundraiser, cook, maid, personal assistant, home and yard maintenance, military service, personal trainer, fitness instructor, emergency workers.

- *Example.* Meagan loves breaking a sweat. In fact, the more physical the work, the more she enjoys it. She is most happy when she is mowing or cleaning gutters for an elderly neighbor or a single mom. In her spare time Meagan volunteers at the local assisted-living home, where she helps elders get to know their computers. Meagan delights in doing what no one else wants to do to make life run smoothly for those close to her.

- *Potential hindrances to success.* Losing joy because of exhaustion or overcommitment; not knowing how to monetize work; doing for others what they *can* do for themselves.

Adventurer. *An adventurer relishes the thrill of discovery, loves to be the point person of exploring uncharted territory, and often loves to be outdoors.*

- *Core motivation.* Seeks to make the world a better place by discovering and recording the unusual or rare; loves to be surprised; loves to push the envelope.

- *Possible pathways.* Explorer, mountain climber, surfer, hiker, woodsman or woman, park ranger, forestry service, pilot, idea person, photographer, artist, athlete, engineer, entrepreneur, missional Christian, church planter, missionary in foreign country.

- *Example.* As a student of anthropology, Jorge hopes to be hired to study the stories of neighborhoods by interviewing their oldest residents. He loves research, especially when it involves talking to people. Over summer break he recorded his neighbors' best stories for a documentary film. In his spare time Jorge is mapping local lava tubes for a university. Jorge lives for the surprise of discovery.

- *Potential hindrances to success.* Going solo and losing touch; needs to remember to invite others along on the journey.

Healer. *A healer relieves suffering of all kinds and instinctively knows how to make the other feel better.*

- *Core motivation.* Seeks to make the world a better place by alleviating any kind of pain.

- *Possible pathways.* Chiropractor, doctor, dentist, therapist, nurse, nurse practitioner, self-help writers, minister, spiritual director, massage therapist, yoga teacher, a person of prayer, counselor, mediator, hospital chaplain.

- *Example.* Belinda is a chiropractor who exercises healing through many avenues: a hot cup of herbal tea, a serene office, soothing music and a soft touch. She notices the pain of others. Belinda has healing in her hands as well as in her heart. Every other year she volunteers for a medical mission in Mexico, where she offers chiropractic care to the poorest of the poor. Helping others to feel better is her passion.

- *Potential hindrances to success.* Carrying too much pain of others while not refilling one's inner well; needs down time and experiences that will refresh body and soul.

Organizer. *An organizer makes sense out of chaos and makes the world better by organizing people and systems.*

- *Core motivation.* Seeks to make the world a better place by reducing chaos and creating systems of order.

- *Possible pathways.* Librarian, events coordinator, household/ office organizer, maid, personal assistant, executive leader.

- *Example.* With more energy to spare than a toddler, Maria loves to make things happen. She coordinates both celebratory and fund-raising events for nonprofit organizations. She is well-known for her unique flair as well as her ability to attract folks to her events. To her friends she is the closet organizer who can get a wardrobe purged and in shipshape condition in an hour or two. Maria's passion is to simplify life by creating order.

- *Potential hindrances to success.* Becoming too rigid and structured; needs to appreciate and give space to spontaneity and art.

Activist. *An activist notices inequities and seeks to make them right, and is commonly heard to say, "Why isn't someone doing something about this?"*

- *Core motivation.* Seeks to make the world a better place by bringing equality and by making life better for many people at once.

- *Possible pathways.* Politician, entrepreneur, religious worker, social worker, political and social activist, fundraiser, environmentalist.

- *Example.* Steven is a lawyer who now works as an advocate for foster children. It is important to Steven that kids grow up believing that fairness is possible. During the Occupy Movement, Steven camped downtown. He even spent a few nights in jail. He saw this as his service to the community. He was proud to be involved as a representative of the 99 percent. Steven's passion is equality for every person.

- *Potential hindrances to success.* Failing to take care of their own business; allowing the cause to define every area of life while failing to maintain one's own private world; easy to lose balance and fall off the edge of normal society.

My vocational preferences are connector, communicator and creator.

They help me to move my "music" from the depths of my soul and into the world. As a connector I find people fascinating and love to get friends together with other friends. As a communicator I love hearing the stories of others and learning from them. I also love to tell stories and cherish situations where mutual learning happens. My creator spark overlays all that I do, including my impulse to start businesses. My three categories describe me accurately and are not too surprising.

The results of the preferences survey should not be much of a surprise to you either. You probably already know what you like to do. Your *how* is meant to help you focus your energy. Naming your preferences establishes a language to help you do that.

Next you will create a grid that will both aid you in making better decisions and focus your efforts toward your vocation.

YOUR *WHAT* AND *HOW* GRID

Begin your *what* and *how* grid by creating a chart similar to table 11.1.[1] Write your vocational credo in the top box where it says, "God created me to."[2] Add your three preferences, your *how*, in the top three boxes, where I have placed mine.

Table 11.1. The *what* and *how* grid

God created me to *help others find their voice and vocation so that they can serve God and community with greater creativity and power and change the world.*		
CONNECTOR	**CREATOR**	**COMMUNICATOR**

Next you will refine your *what*. Ultimately your *what* answers the question, What am I doing to express my vocation? It is akin to a corporate mission statement, which describes what a company does to accomplish their *why*. It is necessary to ruthlessly analyze all of the activities you are currently committed to doing. This means all of your activity outside of your most private life. On a separate piece of paper, make a list comprising every work that you do, every volunteer commitment that you have and every hobby.[3] There is no need to include running errands, doing laundry, washing the car and other maintenance chores unless it is your job. But do include something you find satisfying, such as attending yoga classes or volunteering to walk your neighbor's dog. When in doubt, include the activity. You will eventually notice what belongs on your list and what does not. Consider each activity and note which of your three preferences it responds to. Transfer the items from your list into the appropriate columns on your chart. Some activities might fit in more than one category. You need only list it once, but underline those items. Crossover is a strong indication of a good fit for you. My chart is seen in table 11.2.

Activities for the sake of personal recovery, relaxation and some family duties may or may not fit on these lists. Don't worry about that too much. These are necessary for functioning in life. The grid is predominantly for vocational and volunteer opportunities. Focus on those.

The first time that I did this, there were a few leftover items that did not fit into any of these categories. They were things like travel, teaching classes I didn't like, speaking engagements that were out of my area of expertise, and serving on business boards without a real heartfelt connection. Most of these commitments did not resonate with my vocational credo either. However, one was too important to me to throw overboard. I love to travel and see new sites. Sometimes I go to faraway places to do my job. Travel is a wonderful perk of what I do. Although it is not part of my credo, it is sometimes required and I enjoy it. So I kept travel as part of my *what*. The other three were put on the exit strategy list. The exit strategy list is your activities garbage can. Activities that need to go away are listed there and eventually jettisoned in favor of activities that more closely support your vocation.

Table 11.2. The what and how grid

God created me to *help others find their voice and vocation so that they can serve God and community with greater creativity and power and change the world.*		
CONNECTOR	**CREATOR**	**COMMUNICATOR**
facilitating a speakers series	oil painting class	executive coaching
feeding friends who live outdoors	collage making with my friend	teaching pastors at the seminary
facilitating spiritual formation	my blog	writing stories
vocational counseling	writing	speaking at conferences
mentoring church planters	jewelry making	curriculum design
entertaining	clothing design	teaching college
cat sitter	small businesses	speaking at churches

If you are like most people, your grid needs to be cleaned up a bit. There are probably a few things on your grid that do not belong. So look at your present life with a critical eye and begin to make some decisions about how you want your future to look. First, what do you need to stop doing? Next, analyze each entry on your chart, asking the toxic skills questions from chapter eight: Which tasks fatigue me? Which activities tend to drift to the bottom of my *to-do* list day after day? Which tasks am I doing that I am not excited about? Are there tasks that I feel coerced into doing? What do I notice about them? Transfer these to your exit strategy list.

Study the items on your exit strategy list. Do you notice any themes? This is important information for your future. Knowing where and when you go off the rails will help you avoid making the same mistakes in the future. I have a habit of getting excited about new projects. My interests are varied. Many projects catch my imagination, and I want to be involved with them. I was invited to start a storytelling group. The possibilities seem endless for a project like that. And, unlike my failure club, people were really excited about it, lots of people. Stories and voice seemed to dovetail quite well. So I committed. A few weeks into it I realized that it would require me to do a lot of back-end tasks like setting up a website and keeping track of finances. On the conceptual level the project addressed my vocational preferences of connection, communication and art, but in practice it was not working to my advantage. So I sent it to the exit strategy list and resigned from the project.

You may respond cynically to the notion of "just get rid of it." Some things can't be jettisoned that easily, and that's okay. But nonetheless, be sure to make an exit strategy for the commitments you should not be doing. You may not have the luxury of extricating yourself from problem projects or jobs as soon as you would like to, but if you don't name it as something you do not want to be doing, you will likely never walk away from it.

Creating a new life is impossible unless you actively pursue a vision for it. Planning is a way to hold that vision. You may have to go back to school in order to live into your vocation. You may have to save money, get a grant or raise money before you can walk away from tasks that aren't in your wheelhouse. Or you might just head for the wild frontier and plunge into the chaos model. Different strategies work for different folks and different situations. You are stronger than you think. Whatever happens, commit to moving toward the best possible you.

So far you have dealt with the activities that didn't fit on your grid, and you have culled out those that do not fit. The third and final process asks, What needs to come alive on this grid? What should I be adding? It's okay if you do not know the answer to these questions. You have made space for something new. Hold that space. You will know when the right addition to your life comes along. Or you can proactively create them. For instance, I knew that I wanted to host a theological discussion for women on the "texts of terror" and a few New Testament Scriptures that seem to be troublesome for women leaders.[4] Because of my rich background in exegetical theology I felt that I could do a good job.[5] However, what I was most interested in was giving other women scholars the opportunity to teach. A few partners and I created a speaker series. It fit well on my grid under connector, communicator and creator. If you find yourself lacking meaning, consider adding opportunities that are compelling to you.

When an opportunity comes your way and you wonder if it might be a fit, ask yourself these questions: Does it allow me to work toward my vocation? Does it allow me to express my vocation through my top few preferences? If you get a no on either of these questions, stop right there and consider the question answered. It is probably not worth your time. If it isn't a match for you, it isn't an opportunity. Ask yourself why you are attracted to the opportunity. Could your interest be fulfilled in another area that is more well-suited to you?

If you get a double yes to these questions, move on to the next layer of questioning: Does it excite me? What is the learning curve? Do I have time for this? Can I do this with excellence? If not, what am I willing to give up in order to be involved? If the responses to these questions are satisfactory, then move forward. If you are confused or uncertain, pray for guidance and then call your mentor board for input. As you guard your time and energy, and limit them to what brings you joy, life will be more pleasurable for you.

Believe it or not, this threefold routine has simplified my life tremendously, and it will simplify yours too. This strategy will allow you to be free to do what you do best and to leave the rest behind. The result is a twofold outcome: more opportunities will come your way, and your work will feel much more like play than work.

Consider the words of William Hutchison Murray:

> Until one is committed, there is hesitancy, the chance to draw back, always ineffectiveness. Concerning all acts of initiative (and creation), there is one elementary truth that ignorance of which kills countless ideas and splendid plans: that the moment one definitely commits oneself, then Providence moves too. All sorts of things occur to help one that would never otherwise have occurred. A whole stream of events issues from the decision, raising in one's favor all manner of unforeseen incidents and meetings and material assistance, which no man could have dreamed would have come his way. Whatever you can do, or dream you can do, begin it. Boldness has genius, power, and magic in it. Begin it now.[6]

Commit to becoming the best you! All heaven is waiting to move on your behalf. So are your friends and family, and people who don't even know you yet. People of passion are impossible to ignore. They sparkle. They create a buzz. They will never want for followers. The world loves committed people, and it is waiting for you to act in accordance with your passion.

REFLECTION AND PRACTICE

1. Note those things that you are doing that need to be edited from your schedule. Record them here:

2. Choose one item on your exit strategy list and devise a plan for it. Summarize your plan here:

3. Tell a few people on your mentor board what you have discovered and what you plan to do. Then ask for input. Listen, take notes and ask for prayer. Prayerfully consider the advice you have received from your mentors and then commit to a course of action. Journal your progress.

-12-

Leaving Behind a Legacy

I just want the world to know I was here." Michele was twenty-seven years old and dying of breast cancer. In less than a year we would be burying her. The young and old, the rich and poor, the religious and nonreligious all care about making a lasting impression. We want significance. We want to contribute. And we want to be remembered. Human beings have a desire for legacy. Most if us want to have the fruit of a lifelong body of vocational engagement. As we age and life begins to slow its pace, our thoughts naturally drift toward this question. Legacy, whether one dies young or well advanced in years, demands intention, planning and trust in the next generation. Older folks learn to let go, and younger folks step up and serve their world. Legacy becomes more important to us as we age. This chapter addresses legacy for those of us who are farther down the road.

Webster defines legacy as something transmitted by or received from an ancestor or predecessor or from the past. Legacy also bears the meaning of legal arrangement. When certain aspects of a will are fulfilled, some kind of financial benefit may result. The root meaning of the word *legacy*, dating the word back to A.D. 14, is "persons sent on a mission" or "persons given something to accomplish."[1]

I like a combination of these definitions. It presents a picture of something bequeathed and then carried on in memory of the one who has died. Eulogies often refer to the legacy left by the deceased to loved ones. This could involve money and goods, as well as attitudes and examples that help the survivors live in a more meaningful way. I like to think of legacy as intentional actions of passing on wisdom, caring and substance to those who come after us.

If I sit on a park bench next to someone and ask the person what is important to him or her, chances are very strong that he or she will eventually get to the sentiment "I want to leave my mark on the world." Most people feel the urge to leave a contribution to the world that endures beyond their mortal existence. Our best possible contribution is rooted in the efforts and accomplishments that vocation represents. A vocation well-lived provides the opportunity to leave something of enduring substance and value. The story of Elijah and Elisha demonstrates a biblical pattern for legacy building. In this story we observe Elijah's three steps of legacy building: (1) listening for God's voice in new ways, (2) giving away power, and (3) mentorship.

GOD'S SUCCESSION PLAN FOR ELIJAH

From the first time he appears in Scripture, the prophet Elijah was having a powerful impact on his world. As a man with "a garment of hair and . . . a leather belt around his waist" (2 Kings 1:8), he cut a striking pose. Everyone who encountered him knew who he was. The kingdom of Israel had divided. Elijah was grieved that syncretism was creeping into the religious practices of his beloved Israel. As a result of pagan practices the entire society deteriorated into brutal dictatorship, inhumanity and chaos. His mission from

God was to right these ongoing wrongs and to call his people back to a pure practice of their faith. Elijah was a man of action rather than a man of words. He had a unique relationship with God that allowed him to experience spectacular, dramatic events: he predicted a drought in Israel, he was fed by ravens, he caused a ceaseless fountain of flour and oil to flow for the widow at Zarephath, he raised her boy from the dead, he challenged the prophets of Baal to a contest of power (and won), he oversaw the killing of Baal's prophets, he prophesied the end of the drought, and he called fire down from heaven, which consumed fifty men. Ahab and Jezebel, the rulers of Israel, seemed to tolerate Elijah—until he challenged their power. They then sought to kill him. A depleted and depressed Elijah ran for his life until he collapsed with a death wish on his lips. After an angel came and strengthened him with food, Elijah set off for Mount Horeb, where he would encounter God (1 Kings 17–19:9). This is where we drop into the biblical text.

> The Lord said, "Go out and stand on the mountain in the presence of the Lord, for the Lord is about to pass by."
>
> Then a great and powerful wind tore the mountains apart and shattered the rocks before the Lord, but the Lord was not in the wind. After the wind there was an earthquake, but the Lord was not in the earthquake. After the earthquake came a fire, but the Lord was not in the fire. And after the fire came a gentle whisper. When Elijah heard it, he pulled his cloak over his face and went out and stood at the mouth of the cave. (1 Kings 19:11-13)

Elijah's world was a cacophony of thunderous clouds, bellowing smoke, pounding rain, life, death, blood, famines, droughts, threats, and dogs and birds feasting on the carcasses of kings and queens. Fatigue and fear, the emotional chatter of Elijah's life, had exhausted him to the core. Yet there he stood in the presence of God waiting for what came next. In antithesis to the drama that he knew so well, God sent a lifeline in the form of a still, small voice. Israel knew God's voice in the earthquake, the wind and the fire, yet this time God spoke differently, in a soft, feminine voice. Was something new in store for Elijah? The still, small voice had captured his attention. Perceiving that he was on holy ground, he veiled his face and stepped forward to receive whatever it was that God would say to him.[2] Although we will never know what was said in the soft voice, we are privy to what happened next. "The LORD said to him, 'Go back the way you came, and go to the Desert of Damascus. When you get there, anoint Hazael king over Aram. Also, anoint Jehu son of Nimshi king over Israel, and anoint Elisha . . . to succeed you as prophet'" (vv. 15-16).

What was that? A successor? By the timbre of this story Elijah was growing weary with the life of a prophet, but I wonder if he was ready to hear the word *successor*. In fact, I wonder if he was thinking past the moment. Nevertheless, Elijah responded immediately with obedience, whether he was ready to hear God's plan or not.

Looking at biblical themes, we notice that anointing with oil was a form of passing power from one person to another. Often power was transmitted from God to its recipients through the hands of the prophets. Since Elijah was neither king over Aram or Israel, he did not pass power to them in regards to rulership of Israel. This power simply wasn't his to give away. The anointing for rulership came directly from God through the hands of the prophet. However, when Elijah anointed Elisha, it was different. The story tells us that he was indeed passing on prophetic power from his own life to Elisha's life, which was a significant transference. In the passing of power, Elijah allowed himself to be shifted, to take on a new assignment that was perhaps less glamorous but was needed if Israel was to survive the ravages of broken leadership and a divided kingdom. The shift was to create prophetic continuity for Israel. Rather than retirement, as we experience it in our culture, Elijah's job description was changed but not eliminated. He became a prophetic mentor rather than the fire-and-brimstone prophet he had been. He was given a new assignment. When Elijah anointed Elisha, he knew he would eventually be giving up his work as he knew it to be. Some say that the mentorship between the two lasted about six years. They worked side by side, with Elisha learning to communicate the voice of God to his people by Elijah's example.

I wonder if Elijah felt that Elisha was ready to carry the prophetic burden by the time Elijah was carried away in the fiery chariot. We don't know much about that because the story does not yield the details of Elijah's thoughts, but as we dip back into the text we will see the story shift from Elijah's perspective to that of Elisha.

> As they were walking along and talking together, suddenly a chariot of fire and horses of fire appeared and separated the two of them, and Elijah went up to heaven in a whirlwind. Elisha saw this and cried out, "My father! My father! The chariots and horsemen of Israel!" And Elisha saw him no more. . . .
>
> Elisha then picked up Elijah's cloak that had fallen from him and went back and stood on the bank of the Jordan. He took the cloak that had fallen from Elijah and struck the water with it. . . . When he struck the water, it divided to the right and to the left, and he crossed over. (2 Kings 2:11-14)

In those six years of mentoring, Elijah had weathered a few more dramatic encounters with Israel's kings and queens; he had trained his young protégé and then off he went in the fiery chariot. An emotional Elisha responds with "My father! My father!" demonstrating the intimate nature of their relationship. "Elisha then picked up Elijah's cloak that had fallen from him." This one statement is so rich that an entire book could be woven around it. Of all the details that the writer could have given us, this one seems relatively insignificant at first blush. But the writer wanted his readers to really think about that cloak and what it meant for Elisha to bend over and pick it up.

In an age of no photo IDs or selfies, it must have been a trick to figure out who was who, unless, of course, a person wore distinctive clothing. I am guessing that many people were known by their clothing, which probably functioned much like our driver's license or ID card. We know that this was the case with Elijah because he is described both in the Old and New Testaments by his clothing (2 Kings 1:8).[3] Elijah's cloak had become symbolic of the role of Israel's prophet.

When Elisha picked up the cloak, he accepted his master's role of great influence and responsibility. This detail was not lost on Elisha, who wasted no time in testing his inheritance. With anticipation he struck the water with the cloak and the Jordan River parted just as it had done earlier that day for Elijah (2 Kings 2:8). One can imagine the self-satisfied smile on the face of Elisha as he tucked the cloak under his arm and wandered off to his very own wild frontier.

Thus, the writer demonstrates that the prophetic legacy had indeed been passed from father to son, from mentor to mentee. Along with it was the promise of God's presence in the life of the newly launched prophet Elisha. When Elisha accepted the prophetic office, he became responsible to convey God's message to the people. He was Israel's truth-teller now. His challenge was to turn the hearts of the people back to their God by revealing to them the darkness of their ways.

This story has much to offer us in regard to legacy and vocation, challenging us to be open to *hear* God in new ways, and to adapt to a different view of our usefulness in later years by *giving away power*. It also addresses the importance of *mentoring*. We will take a closer look at each of these and discover how they might be expressed in our contemporary context.

> It is quite true what philosophy says, that life must be understood backward. But then one forgets the other principle: that it must be lived forward.
>
> SØREN KIERKEGAARD[4]

HOW LEGACY BUILDS ON VOCATION

The work that you have done thus far to discover your vocation will give you the ability to live an intentional life. Legacy is built on that intentionality. For the sake of discussion let's agree that your body of work will be one that can be passed on. Much like Elijah's passion, the very nature of the work we do vocationally is meant to ignite those who come after us.

You have become a good listener. You have listened to your inner child to discover your first wound. You have named your favorite quote, leading you to your enduring values. You have listened to what your heart is telling you to do about the world's great needs. You have listened to your inner dialogue, discovering your own barriers to success and your toxic skills. In summation, you have listened for the call to the wild frontier. There is one last *listen* to learn. Like Elijah, we must learn the flexibility of listening in unexpected ways for unexpected direction.

When my children were young, it was not uncommon to have a house full of neighbor kids. These were cousins, friends and strays who came from just as many different backgrounds. Family rules differed from home to home, making it difficult to keep order under our roof when the house was full of children's voices. My husband and I came up with a plan for success. We sifted the rules down to one primary command: *Listen and obey.* There were a few others, such as respect others and do no physical harm. But listen and obey was the rule the kids could default to in times of confusion. It was the rule invoked the most often. With that, the kids' only job was to keep their ears tuned to us. A short list of rules made it possible for the kids to be successful.

As followers of Jesus it is the same for us. We have one job and one job alone. That is to listen for God and take to heart what God says—a soft heart. Listening to God stills the inner critic. No matter how wild or seemingly unconcerned we fancy ourselves to be, we all have a tough inner critic that can thwart success. By listening we learn to accept reality as it is rather than as we think it is.

In his book *Nudge* Leonard Sweet suggests that God is continually speaking to us through our five senses: taste, touch, smell, sound and sight.[5] We are familiar with communication that engages our ears and our tongues. But how do we listen with our hands, our noses, our taste buds, and what would we notice then?

I want to learn how to listen in as many ways as God has to communicate to me, which is probably more than I can think of. A rather enigmatic example comes to mind. I was walking to the Amtrak station and was about to miss the train. Pulling my suitcase behind me I began to sprint toward the station. A bedraggled, shabbily dressed man stepped out of a doorway right into my path. I came to a screeching halt so close to him that I nearly knocked him down. He looked me squarely in the eyes, and then he began tapping his wristwatch, saying, "You are *not* late. You are just on time. You are always just on time for me." With that, he withdrew back into the doorway. For a moment I was frozen. *What was that all about? Is he crazy?* Yet his words carried a weight that I could not explain. They stuck inside my soul. Like gum on the bottom of my shoe, I couldn't scrape it away.

As I boarded the train I remembered that in my morning prayers I was stressing over being so far behind on my commitments. I had begged God to help me change my habits of procrastination and overcommitment so I could pace my vocational projects. This problem has been a lifelong theme for me. I was often overwhelmed by deadlines, and important things often ended up in a pile at the last minute. And then it dawned on me: I had just heard the gracious and comforting voice of God delivered by a homeless man or an angel, who knows? By the way, the train was late, so I was indeed just on time.

Listening in new ways—how could that look? Do the seasons speak? Do the rhythms of the ocean speak? What about the darkness? Does the scent of a rose have anything to say to you? How can you practice listening to God in new ways?

REFLECTION AND PRACTICE

Consider the vocational work you are doing right now that would benefit from God's encouragement. Explain your discouragement.

Close your eyes and envision this scene: Jesus is coming to be with you and a collection of your friends. This could be at your church, your home or at the beach. Everyone gathers for the experience of a lifetime, and you all wait. When Jesus finally walks through the door, he pauses, surveying the crowd. As he notices you, his penetrating gaze meets your eyes. He moves through the crowd gently. Everyone wants to touch him; they try to stop him, but he is not deterred. He walks straight to you and takes your hand. His eyes are warm and full of compassion. He leans over and whispers in your ear. You can smell the day's dusty journey on his clothes; you feel the heat of his sun-drenched skin. The smell of sheep overwhelms you. As he leans in to whisper in your ear, you can feel his heartbeat.

1. What does he say to you?

2. Imagine what he whispered. What words of encouragement did you hear?

3. Write them here:

ANOINT ELISHA TO SUCCEED YOU AS PROPHET

For most of my life I have not been able to figure out why anyone would want to retire. Although I do not oppose the notion of an extended, extravagant vacation, it seems self-indulgent to hop into a behemoth RV and tour the countryside limitlessly for the purpose of self-delight alone. Coupled with that thought is the idea that I feel like I am just getting started doing what God has called me to do, which is to help others find their voice and thus their vocation. I want to change the world—not by myself but with others. So I don't want people like you to retire either. We can still change the world. Maybe this is just optimism speaking, but I believe that if we are not dead, it is not too late. This thought leads me to Elijah and what he did in his "retirement years."

When Elijah anointed Elisha, there was a power transfer. Elisha knew that Elijah was committed to train him to carry that power. This was the work of mentoring and legacy building. As soon as Elijah was gone from the earth, we see Elisha commit an act of power by parting the Jordan River just as his mentor had. This was a symbol to the company of prophets that were standing afar watching the fiery chariot scene unfold (2 Kings 2:7). They were witnesses that Elisha would walk in the ways of his mentor.

The younger generations need older folks to stay engaged. As one twentysomething congregant said to me while I was pastoring, "I know it is hard for you right now, but don't give up. We are all watching you." I had no idea that my struggles were so apparent. But they were learning their life lessons by observing my struggle and pain with leadership and midlife. The challenges that midlife brings are not pretty. Midlife is a season of loss and letting go. Financial demands may diminish freedom as folks become sandwiched between their children's college expenses and extended care duties for their aging parents. Health problems may rear their ugly heads. Job and income insecurity may loom large at the edges. If none of these are snapping at the feet of those in midlife, the realization that time is running out certainly will. But midlife folks have learned toughness and tenacity, and that makes us malleable in the hands of God.

God desires to repurpose us from being outwardly powerful to inwardly powerful. This process is exacerbated when we give our power away. We accept an assignment that flexes with our energy levels and our resources. Eventually our children leave home and hopefully are off the financial radar. The house is nearly paid off and debt is reducing. Physical energy has not decreased so much and health is often still good enough. We often have a deeper sense of self and know how we want to show up in the world. We are in a great position for the wild frontier (see chap. 3) and God will repurpose us if we allow it.

REPURPOSING AND UPCYCLING

Remember Bob who runs the El Salvadorian orphanage (see chap. 6)? He relinquished excellent pay, power and prestige. He now mentors leaders and orphans. He allowed himself to be repurposed for God's kingdom. Vocation is meant to continually repurpose us. Except that rather than decreasing in value, such as our recycling programs do with leftover items, our value actually increases and we are upcycled. Recycling programs are more accurately called downcycling, which ultimately means for all our efforts the stuff will eventually end up in the landfill anyway. Reams of white computer paper become paper cups, which then become egg cartons, and when they die they go to the dump. Upcycling is the process of refinement, where the object increases in value. Check out the Pinterest or Etsy websites, where we find the most useless objects that have been upcycled into interesting and unique art.

God is interested in upcycling each of us. The job change that calls us to mentor those coming after us is actually a most valuable and influential position. Elders in the body of Christ help the younger generation interpret the peaks and valleys in life. We are called on to help them discover thin places, places where the veil between heaven and earth becomes so transparent that we can almost reach through to the other side. These are times when it is easy to miss the nearness of God. As sage followers of Jesus we recognize these times and bring them to their attention, and thus we bring God to their lives. Most important, we are called to train them to take the gospel into the future. We will leave the church in their hands someday. They must be prepared.

One of the more difficult challenges of this shift is that those who have power are reluctant to give it up. What often doesn't become obvious until after the power has been ceded is that the younger generation is ready to receive that power much sooner than we thought possible. It is healthy for both older and younger folks when elders pass power on to young leaders. By inviting them to the theological table, as well as the leadership table, and allowing them to challenge and change our theology, we encourage and build strong leaders who are not frustrated. Each generation has a distinctive voice for their cultural context and time. What might not seem right to an elder might be exactly what God wants the younger generation to hear. They know their own, and they know God in ways the elders do not.

THE FORTRESS OF CERTAINTY

Everyone knows that one of the major downfalls of getting older is inflexibility. Our joints and muscles stiffen, making movement less fluid and physical surprises more dangerous. Not only do our bodies have trouble moving quickly but it is not uncommon for our theology to become well-formed, predictable dogma. We have unspoken presuppositions that color our beliefs as well. I call holding to rigid dogma/theology hiding in the "fortress of certainty." Tension occurs when the fortress is threatened by challenges. These challenges feel uncomfortable at best and evil at worst.

Imagine, if you will, five conjoined towers ten stories tall. Windows ring the top floor only. People gather to admire its beauty as the morning and evening sun glint off of its stainless steel siding. Those sitting at the top offer their blessings to those below. There exists a darker side though. These towers are impenetrable, no one can ascend. There are no doors, elevators or stairs to enter, because those sitting at the top have built this fortress around themselves. Problematically, those in the tower cannot leave unless they jump out the window. This would prove fatal unless they have cooperation from those below.

We each have a fortress of certainty that we need help escaping. In seminary we are taught to develop cohesive and consistent worldviews through our understanding of theology. The problem arises when we begin to believe that our theology is as inspired as the Bible is. Someone once said to me, "I can agree with anything that goes along with the Word [i.e., the Bible]." At first I thought, *Wow, this person is really spiritual!* Then I thought better. What if this person's interpretation of the Bible is incorrect? Everyone holds elements of theology in their fortress that are quite plainly wrong. Each of us will be theologically incorrect until we enter the pearly gates.

The mentoring process requires a kind of hospitality that creates vulnerability and trust for both parties. Can you allow yourself to be open enough to be changed by the other person? Can you ask him or her to help you out of your fortress of certainty? I am not asking you to shed your entire theology, maybe just a few bits of it. The health of the future leaders you know depends on your flexibility.

REFLECTION AND PRACTICE

Think about these questions:

1. A spirit of inquiry goes a long way. What do you think might happen if you were to ask a teen friend to teach you about his or her culture?

2. In what ways might you allow a friend to lead?

3. At the heart of legacy is trust, trust that his or her generation will value what you leave. How will you learn to trust each other?

Respond to these questions:

4. What needs to happen for you to feel comfortable with the transfer of power?

5. Describe your theological fortress of certainty to someone of another generation. Allow the person to ask questions and to describe his or her wonderings. Then ask the person respectful questions about his or her cultural context and theology.

OUR EXPONENTIAL POTENTIAL

An ancient Chinese proverb says, "Who teaches me for a day is my father for a lifetime." A teacher who makes an impact becomes a father or a mother. Vocational DNA, passion and wisdom are passed on to the next generation through parenting. Gandhi was a mentor to the world. He said, "Be the change you want to see." These seven little words of wisdom have infiltrated our culture. Just this week I read it in a book, noticed it emblazoned on the side of a city bus and heard it mentioned on a talk show. And rather than becoming trite, these words continue to be powerful. Why? Because they challenge us personally to grow into human beings who do and become good. We want to know our purpose, which is supposed to be our gift to the world. Gandhi's words compel us forward in that quest.

My friend Jordan called me the other day to say thank you. He moved out of state last year, and we do not have the opportunity to talk very often. He now has an interesting and expanding career and a new wife. But he has not forgotten the many hours that we spent together, nor has he forgotten the hard times we walked through together. He said something that brought tears to my eyes, "You will be a part of our family stories forever. My kids will know your name." I feel like Simeon, "Lord, now let your servant depart in peace," because this is what life and a vocation well lived is all about for me. What did I do for Jordan? Mostly I just listened and delighted in him. And I promised him that everything was going to work out. I am so glad that it actually worked out.

Peter Sellers's last movie is *Being There.*[6] As Chance, an intellectually challenged gardener, he was catapulted to high society by sheer accident when his employer died. He dressed so people assumed he was somebody important. He repeated simple TV-informed phrases that were mistaken for sage bits of wisdom. He never said much, not more than a few words at a time. Nobody knew the depth of his disability. This movie reminds me of a proverb, "Even fools are thought wise if they keep silent, / and discerning if they hold their tongues" (Proverbs 17:28). Chance played the silence card, and he was mistaken for something he wasn't. The point being that a sage listener goes a long way. The fewer words the better. We may never know the depth of what we pass on, even though it might be the simplest of concepts. The Jordans of the world will gather wisdom as needed. Seed planting bears fruit, and seeds produce after their kind. Most seeds are very small. Legacy is transmitted through encounters of heart as we plant the seeds of wisdom and water them with a listening posture. The best we as elders can do is to trust this process.

As I approached my fifties it became increasingly important to me to mentor leaders. I realized that the reward for me at this stage of my career was to reproduce my passion for voice exponentially (me times five at a time) rather than by addition (me plus one, plus one and so on). If I could mentor five leaders at once and they could subsequently mentor five each, then in two seasons of training, thirty people would be mentored into leadership instead of two.

After retiring from the pastorate, I began to teach in classrooms, churches or wherever I was given opportunity. Multiplication was my focus. I taught pastors who then influenced their congregations. It was exponential growth. I have since chatted with many people in this similar stage of life who have done the same. As we age, we look for ways that accelerate our influence and build our legacy.

Nothing should keep younger folks from doing the same. They must be invited to share their passion with anyone who will listen. If the Silicon Valley explosion of creativity and innovation, mostly accomplished by the twenty- to thirty-five-year-old demographic, has taught us anything, it is that our young people are one of our strongest resources.

There is no magic age when one should graduate from addition to multiplication. It should happen when you discover that you carry a unique message. And guess what? That would be your vocational credo. If you have done the "Reflections and Practices" in this book, you will be on your way to developing your unique voice. Look for opportunities to speak up, to participate and to grow your passion. The sooner, the better.

We have discussed the importance of listening for God in new ways and the need to pass on power, and we have observed several stories of mentoring. How might each of these in their own way create a legacy in your life?

Reflect on this poem penned by Dawna Markova.

> I will not die an unlived life.
> I will not live in fear
> of falling or catching fire.
> I choose to inhabit my days,
> to allow my living to open me,
> to make me less afraid,
> more accessible,
> to loosen my heart
> until it becomes a wing,
> a torch, a promise.[7]

REFLECTION AND PRACTICE

1. Describe your mentoring practices. How will you create legacy as a mentor?

2. Given your vocational credo, what legacy would you like to leave behind? What themes in Markova's poem resonate with this last chapter?

3. What fruit will you have brought to the world when your days are done?

Giving Voice to Your Song

I stand hypnotized on the salty shore
Water exploding here and then over there,
Huge liquid mountains crash against each other in slow motion.
Sea-foam drifts high against the azure sky.
Time stands still as I keep watch over these pacific waves.
There is freedom here
And I sing . . . Out Loud.
Nobody wants to hear me sing,
Even my little granddaughter says, "Please stop!"
But I feel approval.
God says, "Sing louder" . . .
God is in the ocean.

DEBORAH LOYD

YOUR SONG, YOUR VOCATION

Have you heard God encouraging you to "sing louder" in the pages of this book? Some Native American tribes had a tradition of singing called the "Song of Life." It was believed that everyone had his or her own song, a beautiful vibration that came from deep within as a reminder of the eternal purpose of one's life. Those who loved a person, let's say a woman, knew her song and sang it to her throughout life. As they sang, she knew she was loved and accepted for her uniqueness. If she lost her way, the tribe would sing the "Song of Life" to her so that she could remember her vibration and get back to her true self. If the woman committed an offense against the tribe, she was brought to the center of the village where her friends and family would encircle her and sing her "Song of Life" to her, reminding her of who she was created to be. Native tradition says, "People who love you do not care about the dark and ugly things you sometimes become. They hear the beauty of your song, they remember your light and know the sweetness within you."[1] Love, rather than punishment, brought repentance. Each person was charged by the Creator to find those who sing with the same vibration so each could encourage the other, walk together and sing to one another.

What a beautiful metaphor this is for one's vocation. The song reminds us why we are here and what impression we are called to make on our world. When we know the vocation of our friends and family, we can partner with them in supportive prayer and positive encouragement, and stand with them for their success. We can sing their songs to them.

My song was nearly snuffed out by rejection, abuse and literal loss of voice. The terrain of my journey from voicelessness to vocation was fraught with land mines. Friends and family came alongside me and sang. My mother encouraged me to be "not the secretary but the boss." She was the first person in my life to give me permission to follow whatever intrigued me. Because of her, my curiosity and imagination now have full reign in my life.

One of my darkest days in ministry was when a young man in

my church murdered his fiancée, leaving behind their three-month-old nursing baby. All that I could think was, *What did we do wrong?* And I wanted to quit. My friend Barb helped me refocus: "You are asking yourself the wrong question. You need to ask yourself, *Did I love them well?*" She helped me put one foot in front of the other when there were no lamps to light the way. She sang a *song of resiliency* to me.

My sage Lakota Sioux friend, Richard, suggested, "Always show up and always have something to say. People will listen to you." He sang the *presence and boldness songs* to me. Although it was extremely challenging, I did it. I sang. More doors are open for me today than I ever could have dreamed.

Then there was my friend Christine who noticed my reckless behavior and suggested, "I think you are bored. You have *got* to figure out how to keep moving forward before you hurt yourself." Her words saved my life in more ways than one. She sang the *creativity song* to me.

When I retired from the pastorate, I was at a loss for my next step. I sought help from Leighton, who said, " I cannot tell you what to do next, but I can tell you that the most important time for a leader is the time in between." I was convinced that my voice was no longer useful to the church. But Leighton sang *my leadership song*, encouraging me to stay in the game and patiently await the future. I do not have a patient bone in my body, but based on his words I waited. Many years later I am singing once again.

"There isn't a man around that wouldn't help you," was Mark's response to my whining. I was failing to get support for a project that I wanted to get off the ground. Mark challenged my negative expectations and helped me to realize that God and the world want success for me. I began to recapture my *song of hope*.

Then there is my friend Deb G., who with a sparkle in her eye quipped, "You can be anything you want to be!" I don't know how many times she has sung my *surprise song* to me, but it lifts me every time. She helps me think about possibilities and look for the unexpected in life.

These are a few of the many ways that my community has encircled me and sang to me when I needed it the most. I am so grateful for them. Without them my life would be less beautiful, less creative, and my voice would not be my own. Turn you ear toward those who are singing your song of life. Who is singing to you, and what are they singing?

> Many people die with their music still in them. Too often it is because they are always getting ready to live. Before they know it time runs out.
>
> OLIVER WENDELL HOLMES

I hope that you have come to the conclusion that your song is not merely the soundtrack of your vocation, it *is* your life and your vocation. The Native Americans' Song of Life is a metaphor for that which impassions you, your *why* in life, the manner in which you long to be of significance and your love gift to the world. The music in you is the vocation that only you can do. It will go undone if you don't do it, and the world will miss the beauty of God living uniquely through you.

REFLECTION AND PRACTICE

Take a moment to contemplate the many ways that friends and family have bid you forward by singing your song to you. Thank each one.

As you sing your song to the world, can you hear your cheerleaders? Can you hear God say, "Sing louder!"

Who do you need to invite to "sing louder"?

CONCLUSION

Our church wrote all of its own music. We did not sing worship songs from composers outside of the church—no Hillsong, Integrity or Maranatha worship songs. Sometimes the songs were developed on the spot during worship; other times they would be written in workshops. Because we did life together, we all knew who wrote each song and what inspired them. Those songs reflected our story as a community, and we sang them with great gusto. What if developing your vocation was like writing a song? As you have been tracking with the reflections and practices in this book, you have done just that! You have written your vocational song. It is a song that you are destined to sing with enthusiasm, a song true for you. And like the "Song of Life," you can share your song with others who can then sing it back to you when you need it, just like my friends did for me.

Below is the good work you have accomplished as you have journeyed with me through these pages. You have

- discovered the true meaning of vocation
- identified how story shapes your life
- applied events of significant pain in your life to your purpose
- specified your dreams that will heal the world
- created your vocational credo
- constructed your vocational preferences grid
- analyzed your life's work
- created a plan to help you focus on your vocation
- developed a plan for your legacy

This work will likely create an urgency for change inside of you. It is a work that will be transformative and enduring. I hope that you will share your journey with others and help them along their way to finding their vocations too.

The following are some final words from Joseph Campbell, who appreciated the human need to experience a transcendent aspect of being alive: "I think what we're seeking is an experience of being alive, so that our life experiences on the purely physical plane will have resonances within our innermost being and reality, so that we actually feel the rapture of being alive."[2]

Even those who have walked a different pathway spiritually resonate with God's plan for a meaningful existence. Campbell refers to "innermost being" with an air of eternal reverence. Could he be talking about spirit, that deep element of our souls, the part of each one of us that relates to our God?

Campbell's rapture of being alive is felt in the daily excitement of living your best story. It mirrors Buechner's meaning of vocation, the place where deep joy meets the greatest needs of the world, and Paul's *kaleō* and *paraklēsis*, called alongside empathetically for the purpose of comfort. Are you ready to sing your music to your world? Are you ready to sing louder? Your excellent contribution will be profound! What keeps you from finding that rapture now rather than later? The God of the universe is waiting to empower you. The world is waiting for you to sing.

Acknowledgments

Even though I love the world of words and concepts, I simply did not think I had enough words in me to write an entire book. But here it is! As I began to write, I understood that it was less about my words and more about the stories of others. Thus this book could be much longer since there was no shortage of stories, and selecting which stories to include and which not to include was difficult. Thank you to everyone who shared their story whether it shows up in the book or not. You all contributed to my understanding of vocation. I offer my earnest gratitude to the many generous folks I interviewed to create the Vocational Preferences Survey. All who have attended my workshops, classes and coaching sessions helped me to develop a language to describe the elements and processes necessary for vocational discernment. Without you all, and you know who you are, *Your Vocational Credo* would not have been possible. I am grateful for George Fox Seminary, Warner Pacific College and the many students who allowed me to test my thesis for *Your Vocational Credo* in the rich learning environment of the classroom.

I will always be indebted to my friend Scott Davison who encouraged me to get this material down on the page. I acknowledge my cheerleaders, Deborah Gohrke and Christine Wood, women of my heart. Christine was key in the development of many of the ideas in this book. Deborah helped me to understand that my voice has value. Thank you for being my friends, praying for and encouraging me along the way.

My mother, Gail, and father, Bruce, are my most longstanding mentors and my inspiration. Gail has been extremely handy in chasing down the details needed to get this book out the door. My dad has schooled me in a sense of wonder that keeps me curious and asking questions. Matthew, my brilliant son, brainstormed with me to write the Vocational Preferences Survey. My daughters, Stephanie and Tirzah, helped with day-to-day duties so that I could write. Alabama, my granddaughter, brought a lighthearted sense of play when I was under pressure with deadlines. Deep gratitude to each of you!

Biggest love and grandest thanks to my husband, Ken, who has been number one in my fan club right from the beginning. A true Renaissance man, he has cleaned, done the laundry, cooked, shopped, subbed my classes and laughed at my jokes.

Warm appreciation to my editor, Helen Lee, who always came with an encouraging word and a sense of excitement about my project. You are the best, Helen! Lastly, I am in awe of Elohim, the creator God, who surprises me with presence and the richness of new thoughts. Praise God from whom all blessings flow . . . and books too!

- Appendix 1 -

The Vocational Triangle Template

My Favorite Quote

My First
Pain

How I Want
to Heal
the World

My Vocational Credo

God created me to _____

so that _____

_____

The Vocational Triangle

Examples of Vocational Credos

The following examples of vocational credos are listed in order of appearance.

- Bruce: to help those who are displaced.
- Stephanie: to create a space of affirmation and belonging.
- Theresa: to help others to be formed spiritually and find joy, both through making art.
- Ken: to pay attention to unwanted humans and to change the mind and heart of the church about the disenfranchised so they can benefit from knowing each other.
- Sue: to help Africans become healthier so they can raise healthy children and build stronger communities.
- Matthew: to help creative people maximize their potential so they can start businesses that make opportunities for others.
- Mike: to maintain "the peace and tranquility of this corner."
- Jane: to bring people to understand the true character of God through thought and conversation.

- Esther: to save her nation from annihilation.

- Worship leader at undergrad college: to curate experiences where human beings can experience God face to face.

- Sarah: to heal others emotionally and spiritually through her gift of storytelling.

Job Title I am a(n)	Vocation My passion is
Elementary school teacher	curating environments for children that inspire their imaginations and curiosity
Engineer	solving problems by tackling tough issues that stump others
Physical therapist	helping people to adjust to a healthier lifestyle so they can live longer and be a blessing to others
Lawyer	teaching equality, justice and reverence for others that promotes greater love and peace in the city
Pastor	establishing communities of hope, comfort and challenge so that all might thrive and feel loved
Pastor's spouse	curating spaces that facilitate spirituality, comfort and challenge so that people can grow into service to God and each other
Author	telling the truth that allows people to live freely outside the box
Cab driver	facilitating moments of hospitality and warmth while helping people to get where they need to go
Event planner	creating pleasant experiences where people can relax and forge new friends while enjoying old friends

- Samwise: to carry Frodo so that Frodo could return the ring and save his world.

- Joseph: to save his people and the Egyptians from the famine.

- Bob: to make a safe home for orphans in El Salvador.

- Deborah: to help others find their voice and vocation so they can serve God and community with greater creativity and power and change the world.

Vocational Preferences Survey

E ach question has two elements that are very different. Circle the letter in front of the statement that is *most* like you. Don't allow yourself to become bogged down with seemingly impossible choices. Pick one and quickly move on to the next.

1. Would you rather
   (F) assist others in doing what they want to do
   or do you
   (H) have an intuitive sense when someone is in pain?

2. Do you
   (B) seek to make the world a better place by getting people together
   or
   (E) think and experiment your way through problems?

3. Do you
   (J) demand fairness for everyone
   or
   (G) get accused of being an adrenaline junkie?

4. Are you

   (A) motivated to make life easier for one person at a time
   or
   (D) energized by turning the world upside down with your
   ideas?

5. Are you

   (B) delighted by developing relationships with others
   or
   (H) seek to relieve suffering?

6. Do you

   (F) enjoy honest, hard work that makes you sweat
   or
   (E) get excited about tackling tough problems that others
   cannot solve?

7. Do you

   (J) notice inequalities and seek to make them right
   or
   (A) serve others with great care so that they feel human?

8. Do you

   (G) push the boundaries of what is known socially and
   culturally
   or
   (B) like to give parties so your friends can know each other?

9. Do you

   (H) care deeply about how people feel
   or
   (E) bring your focus to the table by possibility thinking?

10. Do you

    (F) volunteer to do work that everyone else seems to avoid
    or would you rather

(C) enjoy think tank conversations?

11. Do you

(I) create organizing systems around the house and office

or

(D) pride yourself in your ability to express ideas and stories that are interesting to others?

12. Is it more important to you

(I) to fight oppression

or

(H) to create safe spaces for people to heal?

13. Would you rather

(I) seek to empower others to do their jobs with confidence by removing barriers to success

or

(C) make the world more pleasant by using color, shape, and form to transform spaces?

14. Are you interested in

(E) streamlining processes and creating efficiency

or

(C) creating beautiful experiences through curated events?

15. Do you

(J) value critical thinking

or

(I) find satisfaction in checking accomplishments off the list?

16. Do you

(G) live as a daredevil

or

(C) have a visionary and strategic outlook toward life?

17. Are you

(H) often told that you have a soothing presence

or do you

(G) find yourself living for the thrill of discovery?

18. Do you

(C) enjoy creating atmosphere without words through metaphors and symbols

or would you rather

(D) help people understand the significance of their lives by connecting the dots between story and spirituality?

19. Do you often

(F) find yourself gladly lending a helping hand

or would you rather

(D) explain to someone how to do a task?

20. Would you rather

(B) help people network to get their needs met

or

(A) advocate for others who cannot do it for themselves?

21. Do you prefer

(E) to think about problems that are deeply challenging to you

or

(I) to solve problems by streamlining processes to reduce chaos?

22. Do you

(D) bring hope and empowerment through skillful storytelling

or would you rather

(G) be the point man or woman when exploring uncharted territory?

23. Is it important to you

(J) to educate those in power regarding social issues

or

(E) to set your emotions aside to tackle difficult situations?

24. Are you more motivated to

(C) forge new ideas in art, music, theater and film,

or would you rather

(H) alleviate pain?

25. Would you rather

(G) be outdoors in nature

or

(F) cook for or feed others in your home?

26. Is it more important for you

(G) to live life to the fullest, adventure is where it is at

or

(I) to help people make better choices by creating useful decision-making processes?

27. Would you rather

(A) help people feel more secure by taking care of their personal needs

or

(F) help others by doing physical tasks they do not or cannot do for themselves?

28. Is it more important to you

(A) to help people to exercise their own choices

or

(E) to become a stabilizing force in community by finding solutions for the challenges?

29. Do you

(J) relish the fact that you can get many things done at once

or

(B) help people feel valued and loved by introducing them to those who can benefit them?

30. Do you

   (A) take seriously the responsibility to help others no matter who they are

   or would you rather

   (H) foster conversations of vulnerability?

31. Do you like to

   (D) get people excited about new ideas

   or would you rather

   (B) organize events where people can get to know each other?

32. Do you

   (J) have a sense of contributing globally when expressing your values in a public forum

   or

   (F) enjoy helping people who are hurting or disabled?

33. Are you

   (B) sometimes accused of being a matchmaker,

   or do you

   (J) find value in changing minds?

34. Do you

   (I) try many different approaches to get your point across

   or

   (A) sacrifice your personal comfort to get issues the attention that they need?

35. Do you

   (C) have more ideas than you could ever accomplish in a lifetime

   or

   (D) seek to transform others through ideas, whether they are yours or not?

Tally your score and enter the total number that you circled for each letter below.

A _____ Caregiver

B _____ Connector

C _____ Creator

D _____ Communicator

E _____ Problem Solver

F _____ Helper

G _____ Adventurer

H _____ Healer

I _____ Organizer

J _____ Activist

List your top three categories here

_____

_____

_____

Notes

INTRODUCTION

[1]Frederick Buechner. *Wishful Thinking: A Seeker's ABC* (New York: HarperOne, 1993), p. 95.

[2]"Matthieu Ricard, French translator and right-hand man for the Dalai Lama, has been the subject of intensive clinical tests at the University of Wisconsin, as a result of which he is frequently described as the happiest man in the world" (Robert Chalmers, "Matthieu Ricard: Meet Mr. Happy," *The Independent,* February 18, 2007, www.independent.co.uk/news/people /profiles/matthieu-ricard-meet-mr-happy-436652.html).

1 WHY VOCATION MATTERS

[1]Logotherapy is founded on the belief that striving to find a meaning in one's life is the primary, most powerful motivating and driving force in humans.

[2]Viktor E. Frankl, *Man's Search for Meaning* (New York: Beacon Press, 2006), p. 113.

[3]Michael Braungart and William McDonough, *Cradle to Cradle.* (New York: North Point Press, 2002), p. 19.

[4]Karl Fisch, Scott McLeod and Laura Bestler, "Did You Know 4.0," September 14, 2009, www.youtube.com/watch?v=6ILQrUrEWe8.

[5]Karl Fisch, Scott McLeod and Jeff Brenman, "Did You Know 2014," February 25, 2014, www.youtube.com/watch?v=XrJjfDUzD7M.

[6]Tony Campolo and Bruce Main, *Revolution and Renewal* (Louisville, KY: Westminster John Knox, 2000), p. 75.

[7]Oliver Wendell Holmes, *The Common Law* (Boston: John Harvard Library, 2009), p. 61.

[8]*The Cider House Rules*, directed by Lasse Hallström, Miramax Films, 1999.

2 WHAT IS VOCATION ANYWAY?

[1]Eleanor Roosevelt, *Tomorrow Is Now: It Is Today That We Must Create the World of the Future* (New York: Penguin Group, 2012), p. x.

[2]Ira Progoff, *At a Journal Workshop* (New York: Penguin, 1992), p. 142.

[3]"Career," *BusinessDictionary.com*, accessed February 24, 2015, www.business dictionary.com/definition/career.html#ixzz2Cn63mQIh.

[4]Frederick Buechner, *Wishful Thinking: A Theological ABC* (San Francisco: HarperSanFrancisco, 1993), p. 95.

[5]Os Guinness, *The Call: Finding and Fulfilling the Central Purpose of Your Life* (Nashville: Thomas Nelson, 2003), p. 39. See also Kevin Brennfleck and Kay Marie Brennfleck, *Live Your Calling* (San Francisco: Jossey Bass, 2005), p. 4.

[6]A. J. Conyers, "The Meaning of Vocation," Center for Christian Ethics at Baylor University, 2004, www.baylor.edu/ifl/christianreflection/Vocation articleConyers.pdf.

[7]*Cognate* derives from the Latin word *congas*, which means blood relative. Cognates are words that derive from the same root word. "Allied by deviations from the same source: belonging to the same stock or root." "Cognate," *Reader's Digest Great Encyclopedia Dictionary* (Pleasantville, NY: Funk & Wagnalls, 1967).

[8]The way in which a person feels a call may be directly linked to the nature of his or her personality. God seems to speak most dramatically to those with dramatic personalities and quietly to those with soft personalities. God may use our personalities as a means to speak to us.

3 HOW PAIN SETS THE TRAJECTORY FOR VOCATION

[1]Ram Das, *Be Here Now* (New York: Crown, 1978), p. 64.

[2]Helen LaKelly Hunt, *Faith and Feminism* (New York: Altria, 2004), p. 55.

[3]"The Wild Frontier" by Randy Stonehill. Copyright ©1988 Stonehillian Music (administered by Word Music, LLC) and Word Music, LLC. All rights reserved. Used by permission.

[4]*The Matrix*, directed by the Wachowskis, Warner Brothers Pictures, 1999.

[5]Helen Keller, *Story of My Life* (New York: Grosset & Dunlap, 1905), p. 182.

4 ILLUMINATION FROM DARKNESS

[1]Xerxes had 127 provinces from the Upper Nile Region to India.

[2]Purim is celebrated every year on the 14th day of the Hebrew month of Adar, which is either in early spring or late winter.

[3]Kathryn Schulz, "On Being Wrong," *TED*, March 2011, www.ted.com /talks/kathryn_schulz_on_being_wrong.

[4]William Zinsser, *On Writing Well* (New York: HarperCollins, 2006), p. 279.

[5]Viktor E. Frankl, *Man's Search for Meaning* (New York: Beacon Press, 2006), p. 113.

[6]*Kaleō* and *klēsis* hold the meaning of "a call" or "to call." They are vocation words.

[7]Giacomo Rizzolatti, quoted in Jeremy Rifkin, *The Empathic Civilization: The Race to Global Consciousness in a World in Crisis* (New York: Tarcher/Penguin, 2009), p. 83.

[8]Dan Allender, *To Be Told: Know Your Story, Shape Your Future* (Colorado Springs: Waterford Press, 2005), p. 92.

[9]Ibid., p. 87.

[10]A larger version of the vocational triangle is available in appendix one.

5 THE PUZZLE PIECES OF YOUR STORY

[1]A claim of the television series *Portlandia*. See "Portlandia: The place where young people go to retire," *OregonLive*, December 18, 2010, http://blog.oregon live.com/portlandcityhall/2010/12/portlandia_the_place_where_you.html.

[2]Generative themes are recurring themes that cause energy inside of us. They seek to address what is consuming our minds, as well as the ills of a culture that disturb us. For more about generative themes see "Concepts Used by Paulo Freire," *Freire Institute*, accessed February 25, 2015, www.freire.org /component/easytagcloud/%20generative%20themes.

[3]For more on the MRS degree, look up these links: "MRS Degree," *Huffington Post*, accessed February 25, 2015, www.huffingtonpost.com/tag/mrs-degree; and "Mrs. America: Women's Roles in the 1950s," *PBS*, accessed February 25, 2015, www.pbs.org/wgbh/amex/pill/peopleevents/p_mrs.html.

[4]Janet O. Hagberg, *Real Power* (Salem, WI: Sheffield, 2003).

[5]Stage three is "Power by Accomplishment"; stage four is "Power by Reflection"; stage five is "Power by Purpose." *Real Power* is a must read for those interested in forming leaders.

[6]*The Lord of the Rings: The Return of the King*, directed by Peter Jackson, New Line Cinema, 2003.

[7]Crockett Johnson, *Harold and the Purple Crayon* (New York: Harper, 1955).

[8]Jim Loeher, *The Power of Story* (New York: Free Press, 2007).

[9]*Tabula rasa* is Latin for "blank slate." It also refers to the theory that children are born with a mind that is a blank slate rather than containing already-formed ideas.

6 DREAMS THAT HEAL THE WORLD

[1]This exercise is inspired by brain writing, a concept from Frans Johansson, *The Medici Effect* (Boston: Harvard Business School Press, 2006), p. 110.

[2]The other 40 percent were not successful. The point of the assignment was not necessarily to succeed but to do something that engaged risk and creativity and to learn from whatever happened.

[3]More on risk and failure will be discussed in chapter nine.

[4]Most Bible scholars agree that Joseph was in jail for about twelve years.

[5]This would have been the equivalent to a father role to Pharaoh.

[6]Terry Tempest Williams, *When Women Were Birds: Fifty-Four Variations on Voice* (New York: Sarah Crighton Books, 2012).

7 CREATING YOUR VOCATIONAL CREDO

[1]For reference, a full list can be found in appendix two.

[2]Saul McLeod, "Maslow's Hierarchy of Needs," *Simply Psychology*, updated 2014, www.simplypsychology.org/maslow.html.

[3]For a look at how the poor find greater meaning in life see Julie Beck, "Where Life Has Meaning: Poor, Religious Countries," *The Atlantic*, January 10, 2014, accessed April 5, 2015, www.theatlantic.com/health/archive/2014/01/where-life-has-meaning-poor-religious-countries/282949/.

[4]Janet O. Hagberg, *Real Power* (Salem, WI: Sheffield, 2003), p. 54.

[5]A. J. Conyers, "The Meaning of Vocation," *Vocation*, ed. Robert B. Kruschwitz (Waco, TX: Center for Christian Ethics at Baylor University, 2004), p. 18, www.baylor.edu/ifl/christianreflection/vocation.pdf.

[6]In Exodus 34:6-7 God describes God's character: compassionate, gracious, slow to anger, abounding in love and faithfulness, forgiving wickedness but punishing the guilty.

[7]Richard J. Leider and David A. Shapiro, *Whistle While You Work: Heeding Your Life's Calling* (San Francisco: Berrett-Koehler, 2001).

[8]Pam Hogewiede is the author of *UnladyLike: Resisting the Unjustice of Inequality in the Church* (Folsom, CA: Civitas, 2012).

[9]Simon Sinek, *Start with Why* (London: Penguin Books, 2009).

9 ADDRESSING THE FEAR OF FAILURE

[1]Robert F. Kennedy, *To Seek a Newer World* (New York: Doubleday, 1967), p. 232.

[2]It seems that someone else has been working on this concept of failure as well. See J. R. Briggs's Epic Fail Pastors Conference, www.jrbriggs.com/epic-fail -pastors-conference-new-name-new-look/09.

[3]Sir James Dyson, born May 2, 1947, is a British inventor, industrial designer and founder of the Dyson company. He is best known as the inventor of the Dual Cyclone bagless vacuum cleaner.

[4]John C. Maxwell, *Your Biggest Mistake Is Not Asking What Mistake You're Making* (Nashville: Thomas Nelson, 2012), p. 24.

10 PURSUING CHANGE AND CHAOS

[1]See the website of "Epic Leadership Center" at epicleadershipcenter.org.

[2]Robert E. Quinn, *Deep Change* (San Francisco: Jossey-Bass, 1996), chap. 1. I highly recommend this book.

[3]Ellen Morris Prewitt, *Making Crosses: A Creative Connection to God* (Brewster, MA: Paraclete Press, 2009).

[4]We started The Bridge Christian Church of Portland, Oregon, in September 1998. We did worship in the dark, with two bands at once, lots of artists in action and dancers. It looked more like a nightclub than a church. We handed out earplugs at the door for the tender of ear. Eventually I started a food bank, and Ken started two more churches for our friends who live outdoors: Home PDX and The Underground. Google "The Bridge Christian Church of Portland" to find magazine and newspaper articles describing the community.

[5]The chaos model is adapted from a conversation and a napkin drawing by Mike Connaway, http://vlife.fifthking.com/portfolios/pastor-mike.

11 DISCOVERING YOUR VOCATIONAL PREFERENCES

[1]This grid is adapted from a conversation with Matthew Loyd, a corporate brand expert and also my son.

[2]The italicized words are my vocational credo; yours will look different. A nonreligious version of my credo is: *I am on earth to help others find their voices and vocations so that they may serve others with greater creativity and power and change the world.* It is my desire that this process of finding one's vocation be

accessible to everyone, including those who have not found refuge in God. This is the reason that I have included a more generic version.

[3]I use the word *work* here along the lines of Progoff's definition in chapter two: Work does not refer merely to "a job that you have to do or a task that is placed as a burden upon you. Having work implies a strong and warm caring, a special interest and concern. It means to be engaged in an activity which you value as something meaningful and valuable in your life, and that you are seeking to enlarge and strengthen" (Ira Progoff, *At a Journal Workshop* [New York, Penguin, 1992], p. 142).

[4]Phyllis Trible, *Texts of Terror* (Philadelphia: Fortress Press, 1984). This book is about women in the Bible whose stories are difficult to understand because of their brutal nature. We studied this book because of an inherent belief that God allowed these stories to be told to teach us about God's character and caring for women. Although the stories are tough, they are recorded for all to read and process.

[5]Exegetical theology is the art of interpreting the Bible from the original languages of Hebrew and Greek.

[6]William Hutchison Murray, *The Scottish Himalayan Expedition* (London: Dent, 1951), p. 6.

12 LEAVING BEHIND A LEGACY

[1]"Legacy," *Online Etymology Dictionary*, accessed February 27, 2015. www.etymonline.com/index.php?allowed_in_frame=0&search=legacy&searchmode=none.

[2]Elijah veiled his face because no man could see God face to face and live (Exodus 33:20).

[3]In Matthew 3:4 and Mark 1:6 John the Baptist is described in much the same way. The Jews would have gotten the connection immediately: Old Testament prophet and New Testament prophet, same voice. Malachi 4:5-6 prophesies the return of Elijah as the indicator that the day of the Lord was imminent. Jesus refers to John the Baptist as Elijah in Matthew 17:9-13. In Matthew 17:1-3 Elijah appears at the Mount of Transfiguration with Moses and Jesus. I would suggest that Peter, James and John recognized him because of his appearance.

[4]Søren Kierkegaard, *The Living Thoughts of Kierkegaard*, ed. W. H. Auden (New York: New York Review of Books, 1999), p. 3.

[5]Leonard Sweet, *Nudge* (Colorado Springs: David C. Cook, 2010).

[6]*Being There*, directed by Hal Ashby, Lorimer Film Entertainment, 1979.

[7]Dawna Markova, "I Will Not Die an Unlived Life," in *I Will Not Die an Unlived Life* (Berkeley, CA: Conari Press, 2000), p. 1.

13 GIVING VOICE TO YOUR SONG

[1]"Song of Life," *Manataka.org*, accessed February 27, 2015, www.manataka .org/page162.html.

[2]Joseph Campbell, *The Power of Myth* (New York: Anchor, 1991), pp. 4-5.

Bibliography

BOOKS

Allender, Dan. *To Be Told.* Colorado Springs: Waterford Press, 2005.

Braungart, Michael, and William McDonough. *Cradle to Cradle.* New York: North Point Press, 2002.

Brennfleck, Kevin, and Kay Marie Brennfleck. *Live Your Calling.* San Francisco: Jossey-Bass, 2005.

Buechner, Frederick. *Wishful Thinking: A Theological ABC.* San Francisco: HarperSanFrancisco, 1993.

Campolo, Tony, and Bruce Main. *Revolution and Renewal.* Lexington, KY: Westminster John Knox, 2000.

Conyers, A. J. *The Meaning of Vocation.* Waco, TX: Center for Christian Ethics at Baylor University, 2004.

Hagberg, Janet O. *Real Power.* Salem, WI: Sheffield, 2003.

Johansson, Frans. *The Medici Effect.* Boston: Harvard Business School Press, 2006.

Johnson, Crockett. *Harold and the Purple Crayon.* New York: Harper, 1955.

Loeher, Jim. *The Power of Story.* New York: Free Press, 2007.

Murray, William Hutchison. *The Scottish Himalayan Expedition.* London: Dent, 1951.

Progoff, Ira. *At a Journal Workshop.* New York: Penguin, 1992.

Quinn. Robert E. *Deep Change.* San Francisco: Jossey-Bass, 1996.

Rifkin, Jeremy. *The Empathetic Civilization.* New York: Penguin, 2009.

Sinek, Simon. *Start with Why.* London: Penguin Books, 2009.

Trible, Phyllis. *Texts of Terror.* Philadelphia: Fortress Press, 1984.

Sweet, Leonard. *Nudge.* Colorado Springs: David C. Cook, 2010.

MOVIES

Being There. Directed by Hal Ashby. Lorimer Film Entertainment, 1979.

The Cider House Rules. Directed by Lasse Hallström. Miramax Films, 1999.

Lord of the Rings, The Return of the King. Directed by Peter Jackson. New Line Cinema, 2003.

Matrix, The. Directed by the Wachowskis. Warner Brothers Pictures, 1999.

Snow White and the Seven Dwarfs. Directed by David Hand. Walt Disney Productions, 1937.

Finding Forward

PERSONAL DEVELOPMENT: DISCOVERING YOUR OWN PERSONAL "WHY?"

Finding Forward is Deborah's organization offering workshops, retreats, etc., to individuals as well as small groups, helping people discern their vocations and how to live them to the fullest.

The participants will:

- find their pathway forward through interpreting their own story
- answer the questions "Why did God put me here? What is my service to the Lord and others?"
- discover how to live out a vocation most successfully
- analyze current activities and learn what to add and what to delete

BUSINESS DEVELOPMENT: ARE YOUR VALUABLE PEOPLE IN THE RIGHT POSITIONS?

Finding Forward delivers a plan to get quality people into the right place at the right time for organizations that wish to more effectively pursue their mission through the development of team members.

Team members will:

- discover their passion and how to live it out most successfully in their work life
- express their passion through their work once they have found the right fit
- develop an appreciation of how their vocations fit within the organization's goals

Organizations will:

- experience new energy and productivity when their people are empowered to do that which energizes them
- become more effective in accomplishing their mission
- increase in favorable outcomes with a minimum of risk to the organization

Finding Forward also offers:

- one-day intensives in personal vocational development
- two-day intensives in organizational development of vocation
- certification training for teaching *Your Vocational Credo* materials
- three-credit college level curriculum based on *Your Vocational Credo*

If you would like to have Deborah speak to your organization, at your conference, retreat, school, or convention on the topic of vocation contact her at Finding Forward: deborahlloyd@gmail.com, or call 503-516-1415.